WORLD BOOK'S

YOUNG SCIENTIST

WORLD BOOK'S

YOUNG SCIENTIST

• LIVING WORLD
• PLANTS

1

World Book, Inc.
a Scott Fetzer company
Chicago

Activities that have this warning symbol require some adult supervision!

The quest to explore the known world and to describe its creation and subsequent development is nearly as old as mankind. In the Western world, the best-known creation story comes from the book of Genesis. It tells how God created Earth and all living things. Modern religious thinkers interpret the Biblical story of creation in various ways. Some believe that creation occurred exactly as Genesis describes it. Others think that God's method of creation is revealed through scientific investigation. *Young Scientist* presents an exciting picture of what scientists have learned about life and the universe.

World Book, Inc.
233 N. Michigan Avenue
Chicago, IL 60601

For information on other World Book products, call 1-800-WORLDBK (967-5325), or visit us at our Web site at http://www.worldbook.com

ISBN: 0-7166-2751-5 (volume I)
ISBN: 0-7166-2797-3 (set)

Library of Congress Catalog Card No. 00-107193

Printed in the United States of America

1 2 3 4 5 6 7 06 05 04 03 02 01 00

Contents

Living World

Plants

LIVING WORLD

The world's largest tree is the General Sherman sequoia in California. It is 275 feet (83.8 meters) high, and the base of the trunk is 103 feet (31.4 meters) around.

All these are living things

Cells, the basic units of life, are the building blocks of all living things. All the different kinds of plants and animals in the world are made of cells. There are millions and millions of cells in your body. They can be round, square, egg-shaped, or rectangular. Other cells live on their own, as tiny plants and creatures. Most of them are so small that you need a microscope to see them.

All shapes and sizes

Among the largest living things in the world are trees! The world's largest tree, according to volume of wood, is the General Sherman sequoia tree in California. It is 275 feet (83.8 meters) high, and the base of the trunk is 103 feet (31.4 meters) around. That's about as high as a 30-story building and heavier than 20 blue whales.

An ameba is made up of one cell. A sequoia tree contains billions of cells. There are all kinds of living things between the simple, one-celled ameba and the giant, more complex sequoia.

You need a microscope to see an ameba clearly. An ameba is a tiny living thing that consists of one cell.

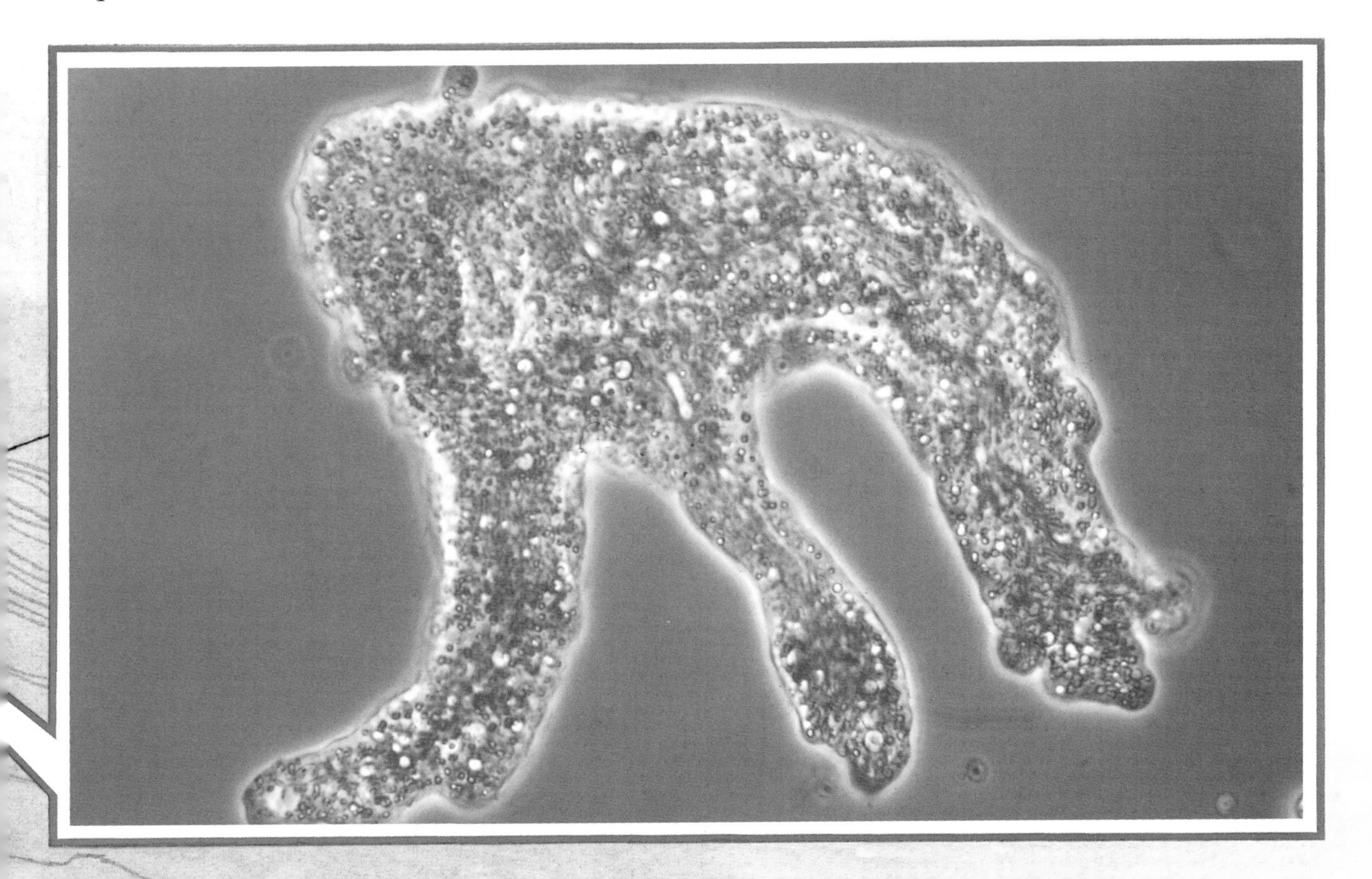

Swans and hares are examples of living things that eat, reproduce, and respond to the world around them.

Look at life

Of all the planets going around the sun, Earth is the only one that has living things on it. As far as we know, there is no other life anywhere else in the universe.

Why is there life here and nowhere else? One reason is that Earth is the only planet with plenty of water on its surface. Nearly three-quarters of Earth's surface is covered with water in the form of oceans, ice caps, lakes, and rivers. Life on Earth depends on water. In fact, every living thing is made mostly of water. Your body is about two-thirds water. A tomato is nearly all water!

Another reason why there is life on Earth is that this planet has a supply of a gas called **oxygen.** Almost all living things need oxygen, which is part of the mixture of gases in the atmosphere all around Earth.

Not all things on Earth are living things. Scientists who study living things can tell whether an object is living or nonliving by asking these simple questions.

Does it eat?

Living things have ways of taking in the substances they need to grow and survive.

Does it respond to the world around it?

Most living things respond to light, sound, and touch. They have some way of receiving information about the world around them, such as seeing, hearing, smelling, or sensing.

Does it reproduce?

Living things make copies of themselves. In this way, the various groups of living things continue to exist. This process of making copies is called **reproduction.**

A sundew plant uses the sticky liquid on its leaves to trap insects. It uses the hairs on its leaves to hold an insect. The plant absorbs nutrients from the trapped insect.

Dividing things into groups

We can arrange everything in the world into three groups. Some things are living now, others were once living, and some were never living.

A table is not living. Tables don't eat and grow or produce young tables! And they don't have eyes and ears or other ways of sensing the world around them.

But if a table is made of wood, then it was once part of a growing tree. The table is not a living thing, but the wood was once part of a living thing.

If a table is made of stone, then it was once part of a large rock. Rocks are not living. They have no senses, and they don't eat or reproduce. So a stone table was never living.

Dividing things into groups helps us to understand how all the different things in the world fit into a pattern.

Scientists who study living things are called biologists. Biologists divide living things into different groups. This process of dividing is called **classifying.**

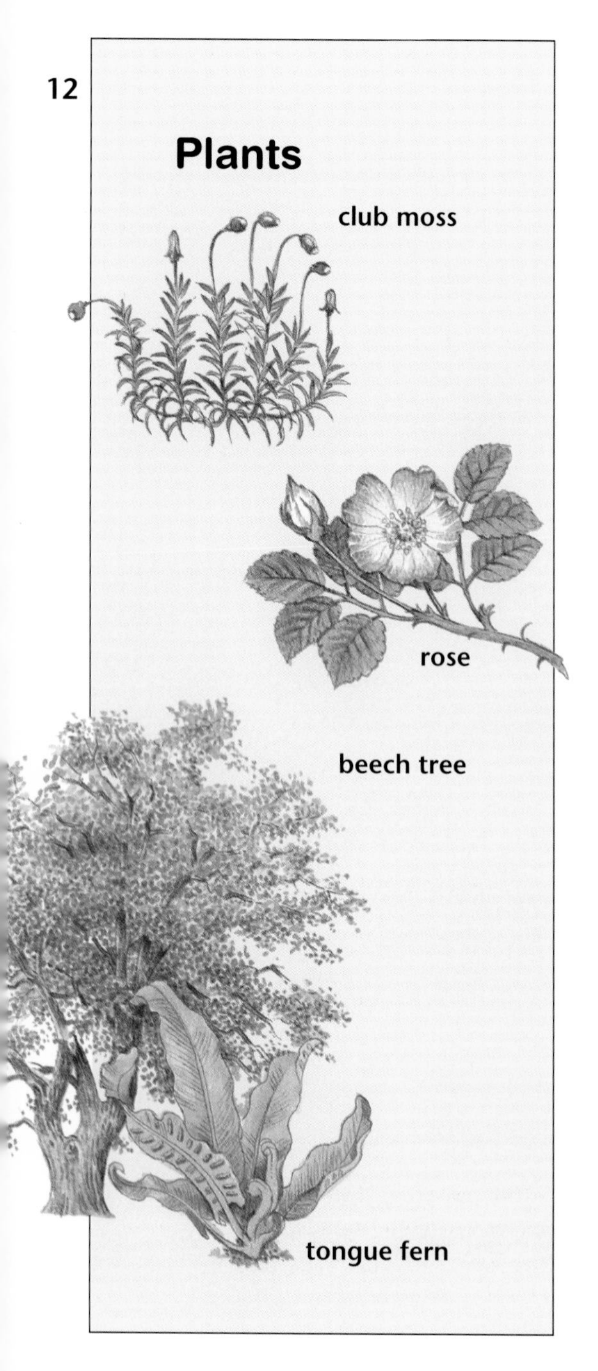

Five living kingdoms

Some biologists classify all living things by dividing them into five large groups called **kingdoms.** The two main kingdoms are those of **animals** and **plants.**

Most animals move around, but most plants are rooted in one place. Animals eat plants or other animals, but plants make their own food. Sunlight helps green plants to make food from water and a gas called carbon dioxide.

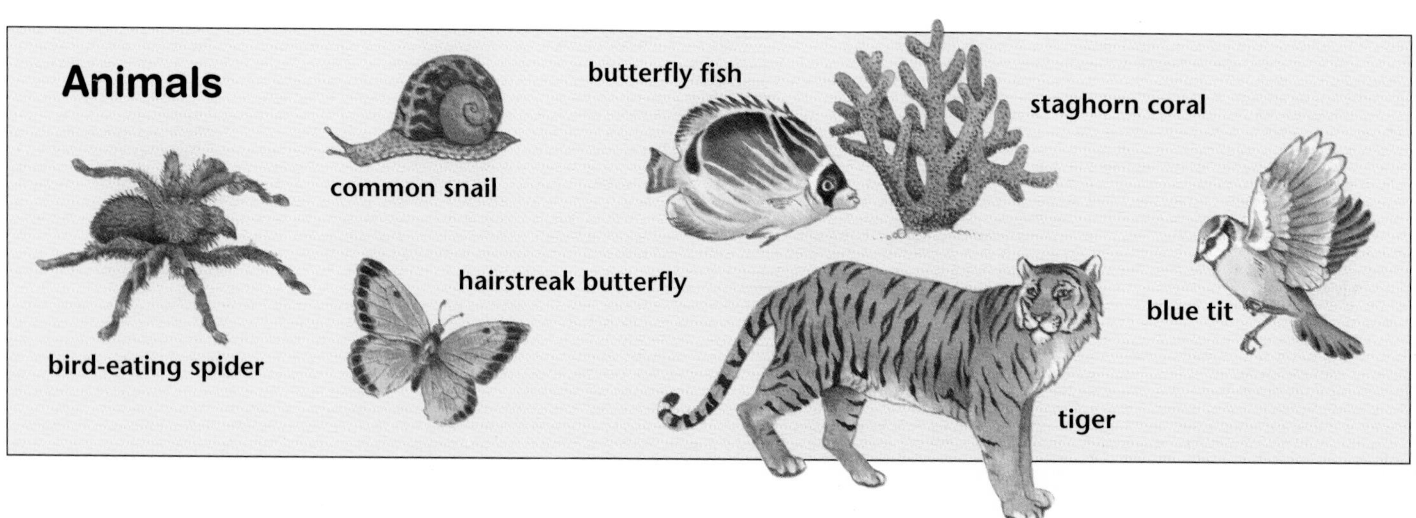

Find out more by looking at pages **16–17**

It's easy to tell that a tiger is an animal and that a tree is a plant. But what about coral? Coral grows in the sea and looks like a plant. But it is made up of millions of tiny animals and eats smaller swimming animals.

Is a mushroom a plant? Mushrooms and other fungi don't make their own food. Instead they feed off living and rotting plants. But they're not animals! So many biologists say that **fungi** belong to a separate kingdom.

There are other kinds of living things that are different from plants and animals. Most of them are so small that you can't see them without a microscope. They are divided into two more kingdoms. One is made up of **protists**, which include the amebas. The other kingdom is made up of **prokaryotes** (also called **monerans**), which are mostly bacteria.

Scientists do not all agree about how different forms of life should be classified, and existing classifications may be changed to reflect new discoveries. For example, archaea were first discovered in 1977, living near deep-sea thermal vents. They do not obtain their food from other living things, and were the first life forms discovered that do not get their energy from the sun. Archaea are classified in the prokaryote kingdom, because archaea are similar to bacteria in many ways. However, as scientists continue to study these and other forms of life, they may decide to place archaea in a separate kingdom.

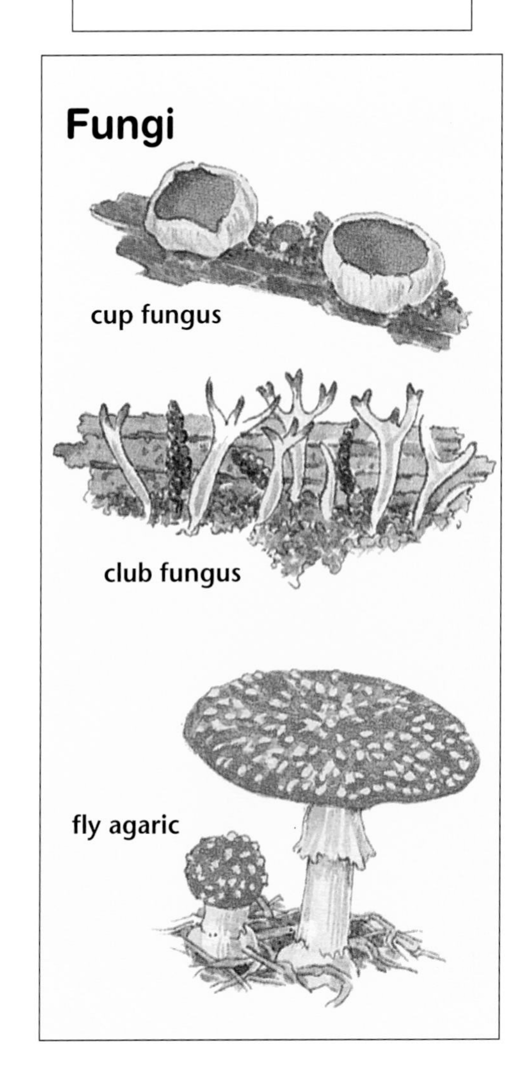

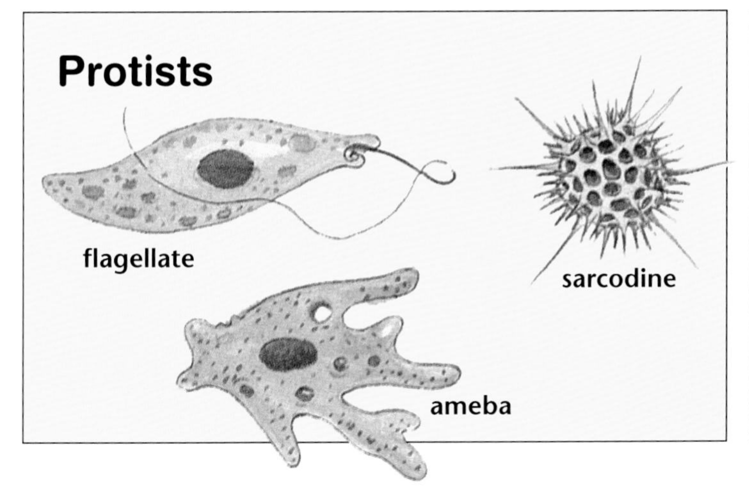

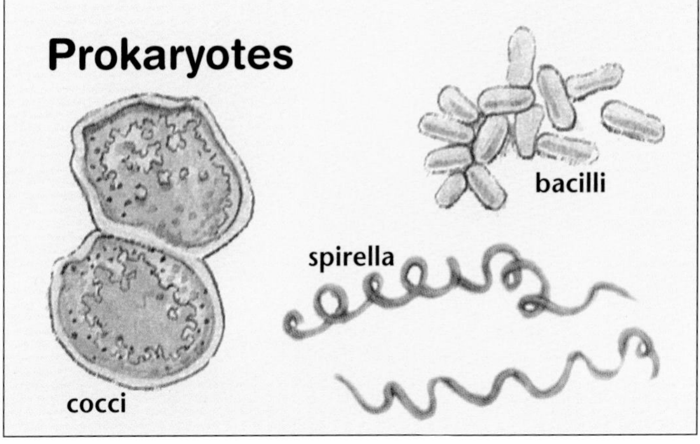

What are these living things?

There are more than 2 million different kinds of living things in the world. On pages 12 and 13, you saw how biologists have classified them into five kingdoms. Can you tell which of the living things on these pages are animals, plants, fungi, protists, or prokaryotes?

Divide a clean sheet of paper or a page in your notebook into five columns, one for each kingdom. Now write the name of each of these living things in the correct column.

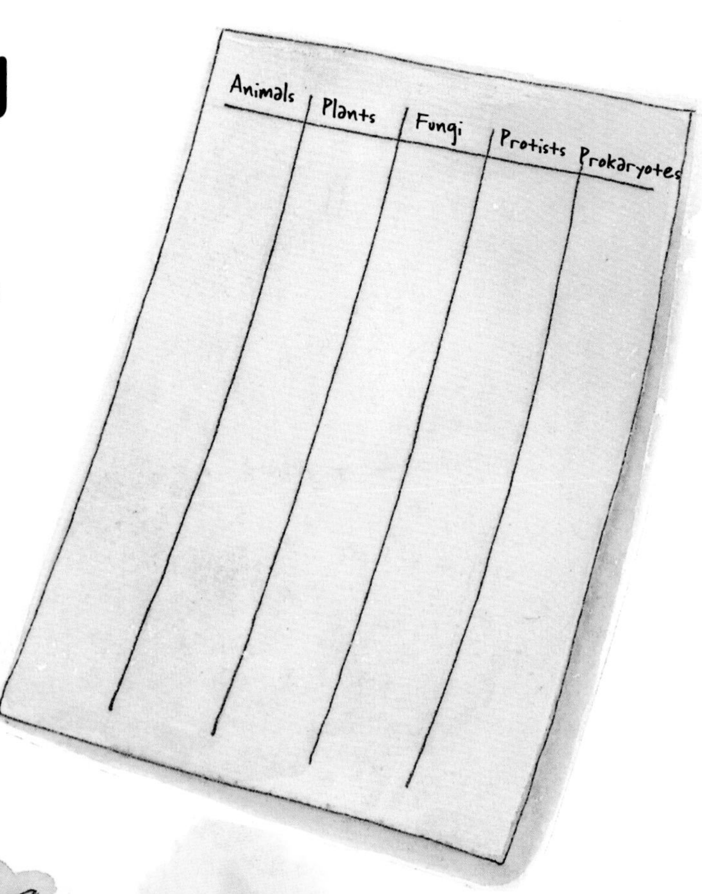

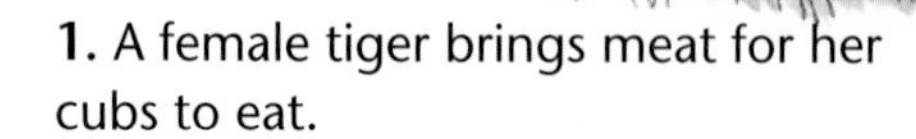

1. A female tiger brings meat for her cubs to eat.

2. Owls hunt at night.

3. Snakes can hear, but they have no outer ear. Their ears are completely inside their head.

Find out more by looking at pages **12–13**
16–17

4. This spider is spinning its web.

5. The sea anemone eats tiny creatures in the water.

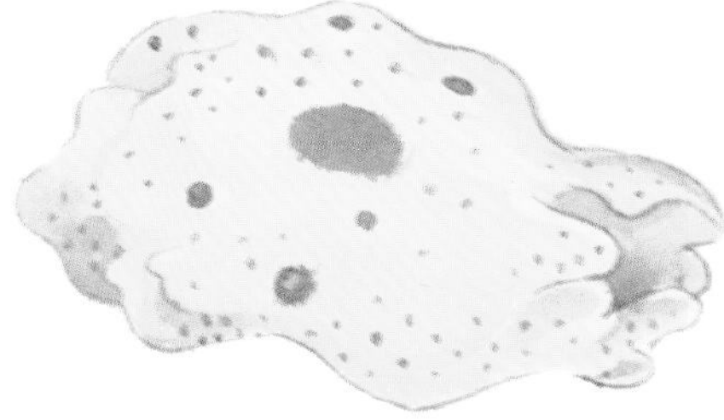

8. Amebas live in ponds, moist places, and in the bodies of animals and human beings.

6. The leaves of this ivy are turned toward the sunlight.

7. These cocci are a kind of bacteria that can cause diseases.

9. Oyster mushrooms grow on the sides of rotting trees, which provide their food.

10. Pine trees produce seeds in female cones.

From kingdom to species

Each of the five kingdoms is a huge group. Scientists already know about more than 1 million different kinds of animals in the animal kingdom, and about more than 350,000 kinds of plants in the plant kingdom. Every year, hundreds of kinds of animals and many kinds of plants are being discovered. But in modern times, many kinds of plants and animals have also become extinct.

It's very difficult to think about such an enormous number of plants and animals all at once. So scientists divide each kingdom into smaller groups of living things. These have particular features in common.

Classifying tigers

Each kingdom in the living world is divided into six smaller groups with different names. Scientists call these groups **species, genus, family, order, class,** and **phylum.** (In the plant kingdom, phylum is called **division.**) The smallest of all these groups is the species. Let's see how the tiger fits into the different groups.

Species

Every tiger is an individual creature, but all tigers belong to the same **species** of animal.

tiger

Genus

Different species that are very similar, such as tigers, lions, and leopards, are part of a group called a **genus.**

tiger

Family

Living things from more than one genus can have common features that make them part of the same **family.** Tigers are part of the cat family.

tiger

Order

Wild cats and bears both eat meat. Meat-eating families make up an **order**. This order is called carnivores.

tiger

Class

Sheep and rabbits don't eat meat like cats and dogs. But all these animals feed their young on milk. They all belong to one **class,** called mammals.

tiger

Phylum

A **phylum** is a group of classes with something important in common. Every animal pictured here has a backbone. These animals belong to the phylum of vertebrates.

tiger

lion
leopard
lion
leopard
wild cat
jaguar
lion
wolf
wild cat
ermine
bear
seal
gorilla
whale
bat
dog
bear
sheep
rabbit
giraffe
pig
snake
peacock
fish
bird
frog
sheep
giraffe
cat
whale
gorilla
pig

Make a model of an animal cell

You will need:

water

a small, solid, plastic ball

a small plastic bag

scissors

four packets of gelatin

1. Ask an adult to help you dissolve the gelatin in some hot water. Add enough warm water to make a jelly that will set. Leave the jelly to cool for a few minutes.

2. Pour half of the jelly into the plastic bag. Keep the rest of the jelly warm, while the jelly in the plastic bag sets. It will set more quickly in a cool place.

3. When the jelly in the bag is partly set, put in the plastic ball. Then add the rest of the jelly. Tie a knot in the bag to seal it and trim off the ends.

This is roughly the shape of an animal cell. The plastic bag is like the membrane. The plastic ball is like the nucleus, and the jelly represents the cytoplasm.

The smallest living thing

Do you know what your body is made of? It's made of skin, bone, blood, muscles, and fat. But what are these made of? Different parts of your body are made up of tiny living things called **cells**. Plants and animals and other living things are made up of cells. Some very small forms of life are made of just one cell. But in the human body there are more than 10 million million cells. Cells are the building blocks of life. All living things are made from at least one cell.

This is a diagram of an animal cell. Animal cells of different shapes and sizes carry out different jobs.

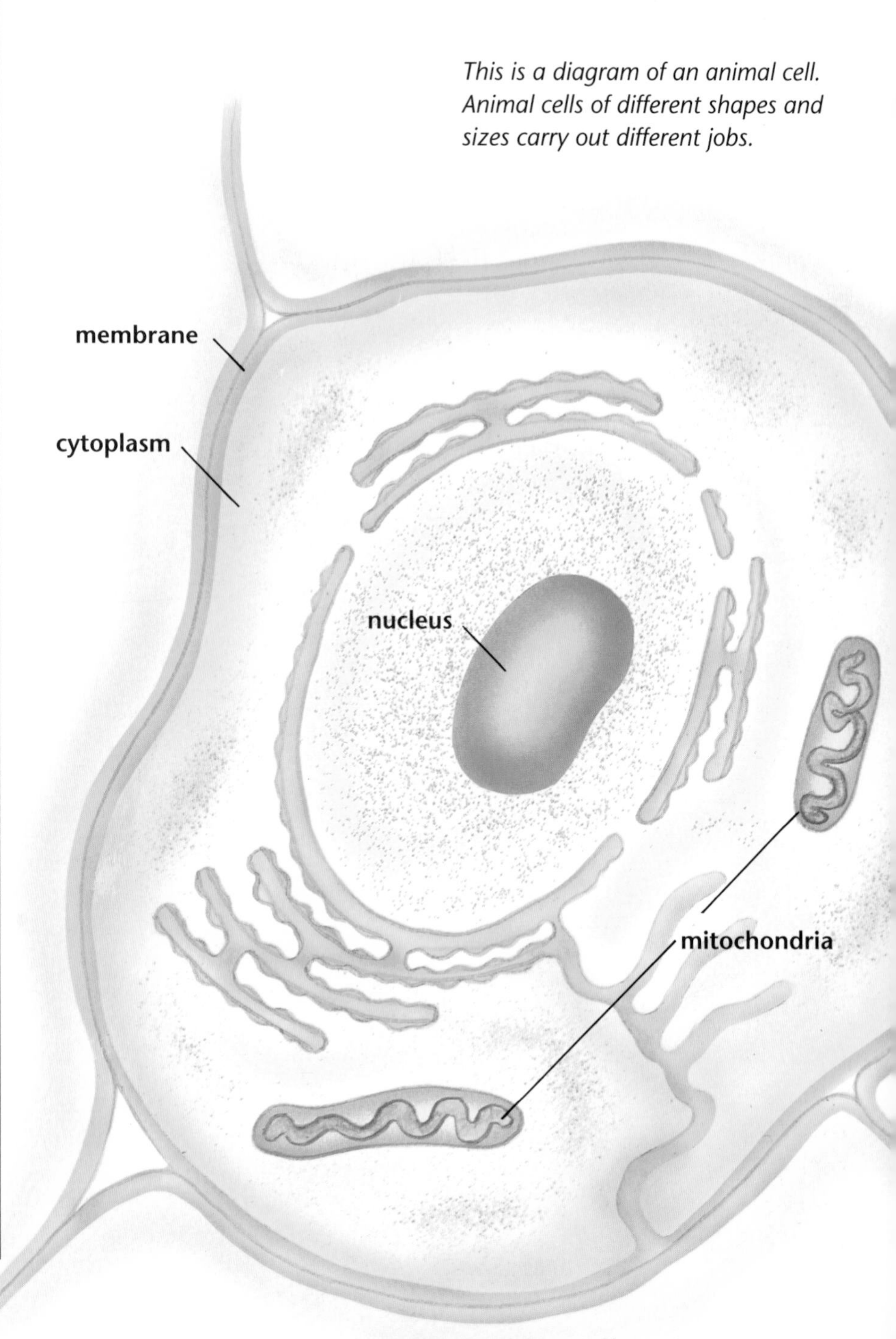

Find out more by looking at pages **8–9**
20–21

What's inside a cell?

Inside a cell is a jellylike substance called **cytoplasm.** This is contained inside a kind of skin called a **membrane**. Plant cells also have another skin, called a **cell wall,** outside the cell membrane. The cytoplasm contains many different working parts and a large number of different chemicals, which all have a job to do in the cell.

The most important part of the cell is the **nucleus.** The nucleus is the control center of the cell. Other important working parts of the cell's cytoplasm are called **mitochondria.** They provide almost all the energy the cell needs.

Chemical substances called **proteins** exist in every cell. They are essential to plant and animal life. Some of these proteins, called **enzymes,** bring chemicals together and help them to react. The chemical reactions in which enzymes are involved are vital to the survival of every cell.

What is a virus?

Viruses are extremely small and simple organisms that live in cells of other living things. Viruses survive by entering the cells of animals, plants, or bacteria. Viruses can make copies of themselves with the help of other living cells. A virus cannot reproduce. It needs to be carried into a living thing in some way. Viruses often pass into an animal's body when the animal breathes. Once inside a cell, the virus uses the cell's materials to live and reproduce. The virus can make hundreds of copies of itself. The healthy cells are taken over and destroyed, which could make the animal ill. Viruses that infect plants rely on insects such as aphids to get them inside the plant's cell wall. When these insects pierce the plant with their mouthparts, they damage many cell walls. The virus can then get into the plant. These insects also pick up the viruses from infected plants and take them to other plants as they feed.

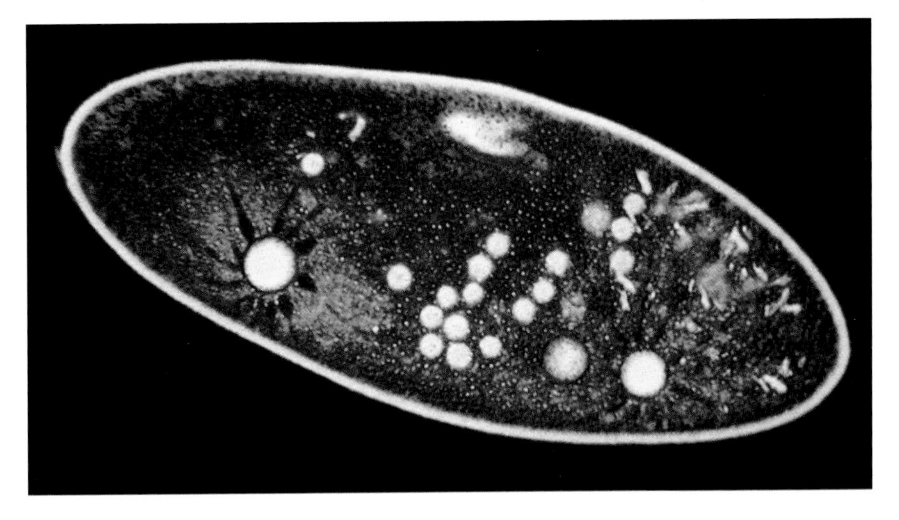

The paramecium is a tiny living thing with only a single cell. It is found in ponds. The paramecium cannot be seen without a microscope.

Find out more by looking at pages **18–19**
36–37
42–43

Life under the microscope

Most cells are so small that you can see them only through a microscope. Even magnifying them about 2,000 times does not reveal the details of all the cell parts. There are thousands of cells in something as small as a poppy seed. So you can imagine how very tiny cells can be. But you can see some single cells, such as the yolk of a bird's egg, without a microscope. The largest cells are the yolks of ostrich eggs, which are about the size of baseballs.

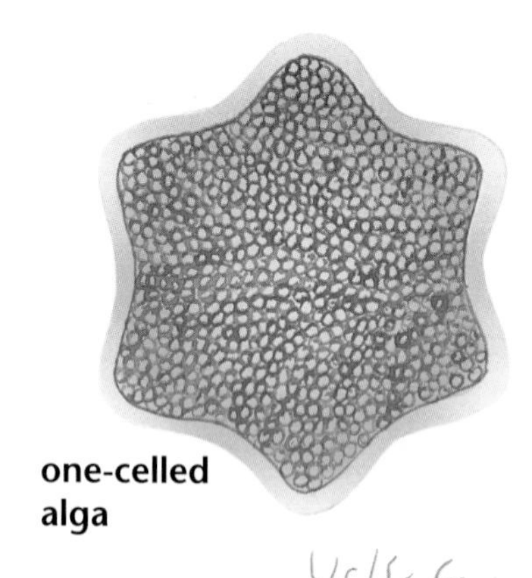

one-celled alga

Cells are different sizes and shapes depending on the jobs they do. Many single-celled plants and animals look like tiny balls or boxes. The cells in larger plants are mostly cube-shaped or oblong-shaped. Muscle cells are long and thin so that they can stretch and shrink when an animal moves. Nerve cells have branches that reach out in many directions. Some help animals to feel different sensations.

Cells are living things that feed, reproduce, and respond to the world around them.

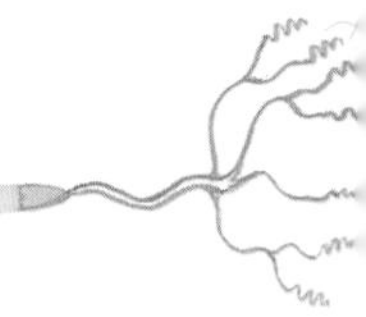

nerve cell

Making new cells

Cells make new cells by dividing into two or more parts. Some kinds of cells, including single-celled animals and plants, split into two parts that are both exactly the same.

Here you can see a plant cell dividing. The cell has a larger nucleus when it is about to divide. The nucleus starts and controls the dividing process.

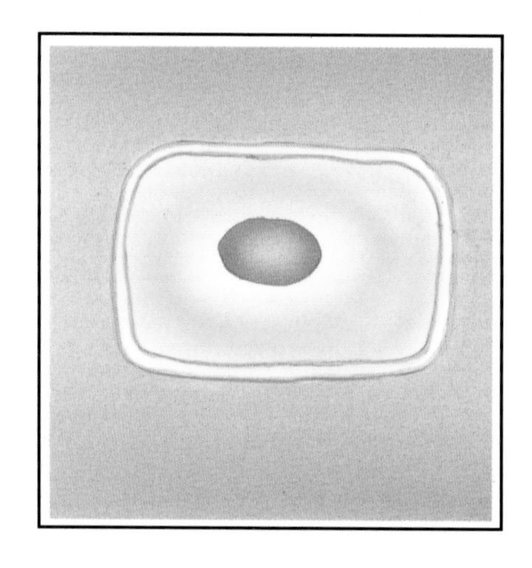

1. The nucleus of the cell is ready to divide.

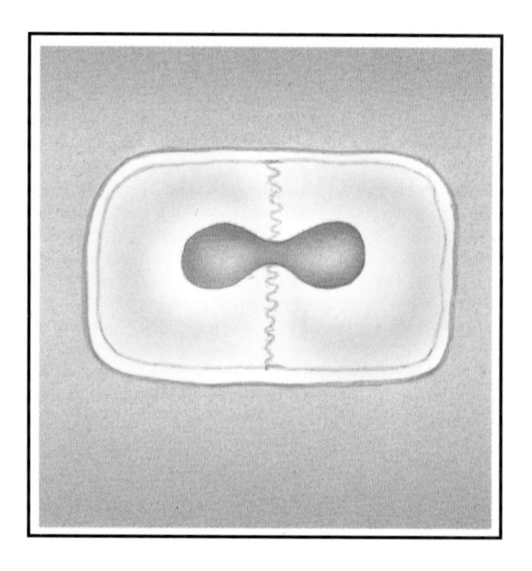

2. The nucleus has almost split in two. A new layer begins to form, dividing the cells.

How does a cell take in food?

Animal cells take in the substances they need through their outer skin, or the cell membrane. This membrane is made up of chemicals that let useful substances into the cell and keep unwanted ones out.

Plant cells contain small working parts called **chloroplasts.** These contain a green substance called **chlorophyll,** which makes the plant's leaves green. Chlorophyll captures light energy from the sun, and this process enables the plant to make its food.

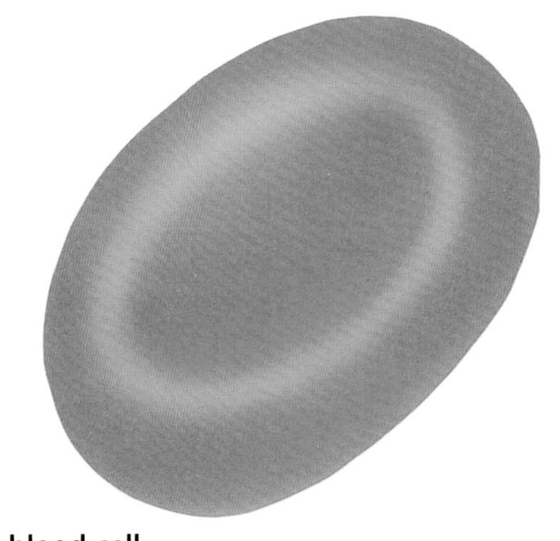

blood cell

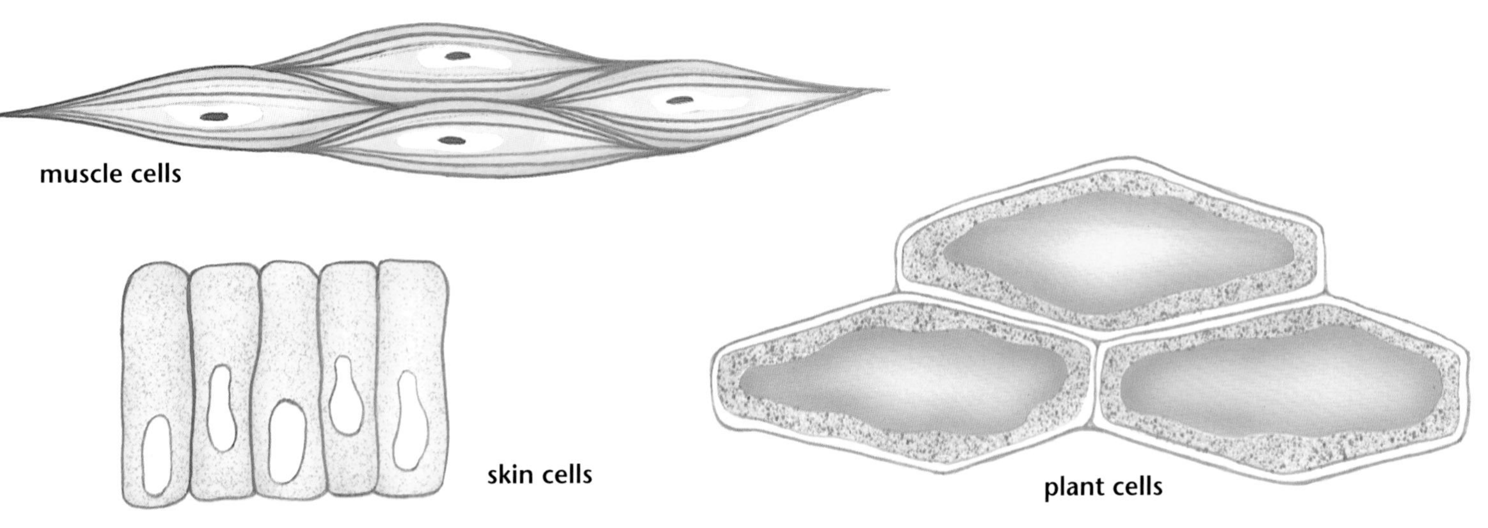

muscle cells

skin cells

plant cells

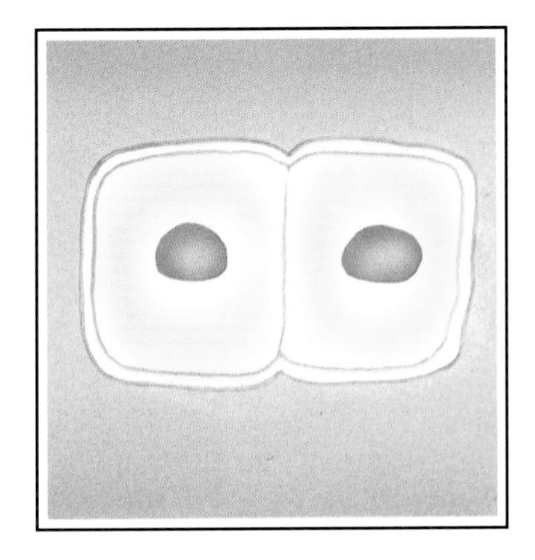

3. The nucleus has now divided into two separate parts.

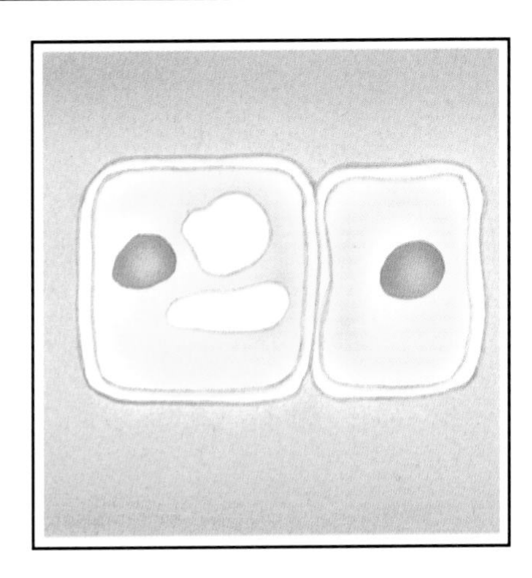

4. The cytoplasm builds up a wall around the new dividing layers.

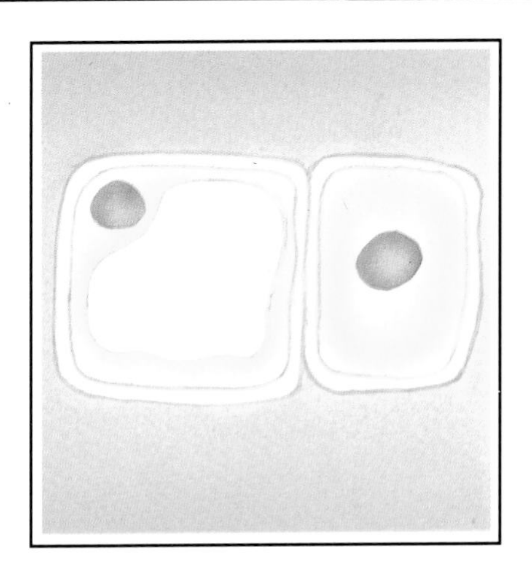

5. The cell has now divided into two separate cells. One cell is ready to divide again.

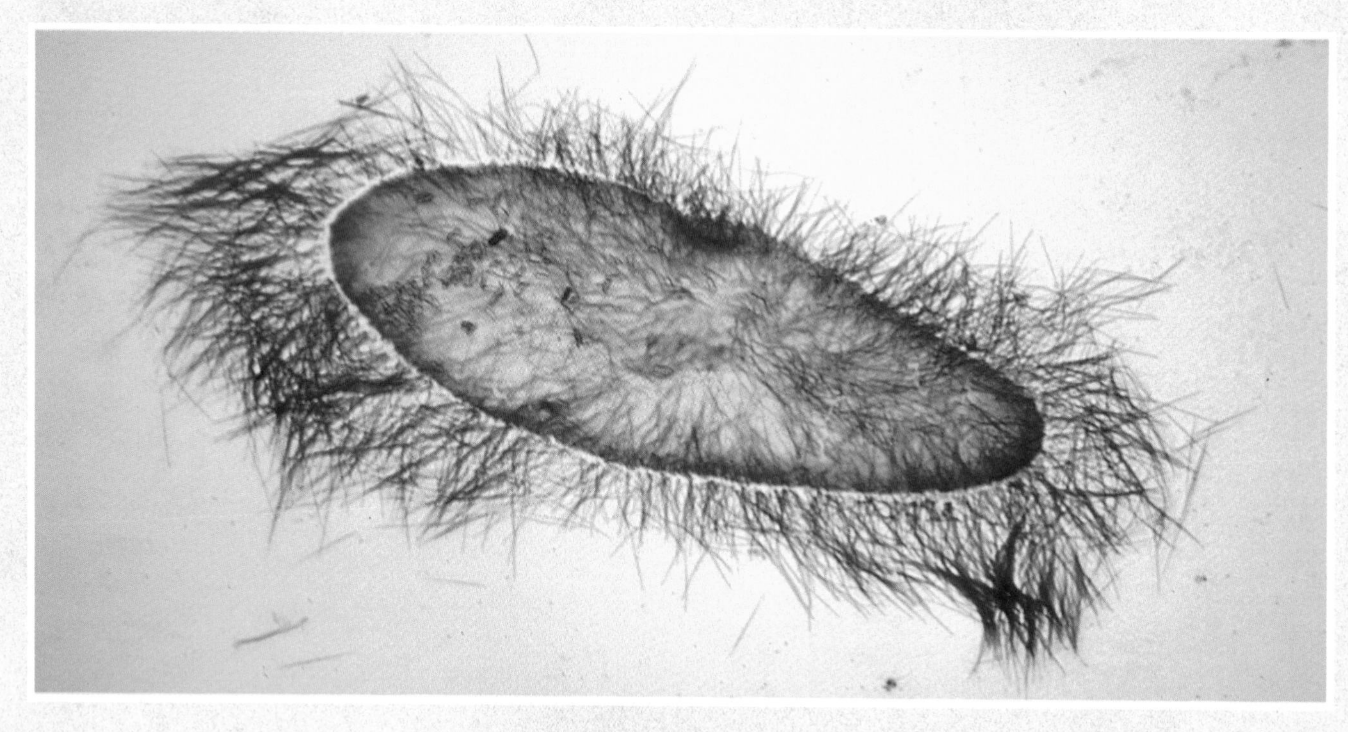

This microscopic organism is a paramecium.

What is a protist?

Protists are small living things that can't easily be classified as animals or plants, fungi or prokaryotes. The kingdom of protists contains a wide variety of different species.

Hairy protists

Under the microscope, some protists look as if they are covered by hair-like threads. These "hairs" enable the cell to move. By moving all together at the same time, they push the cell along. Biologists call these threads **cilia** and name the organisms **ciliates.**

One kind of ciliate is called a **paramecium.** It is only a single cell, but it has a kind of mouth and stomach to eat and digest its food.

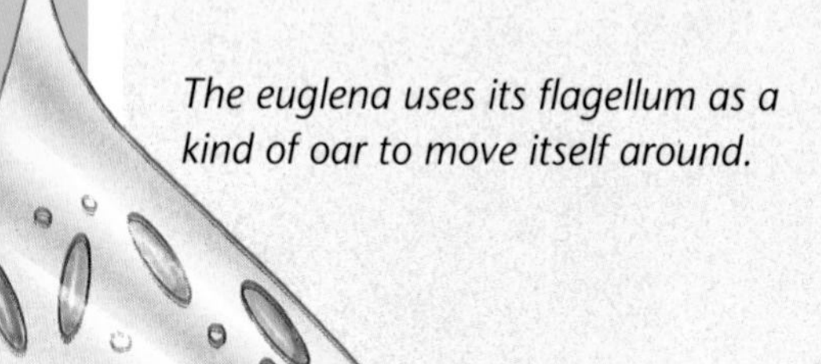

The euglena uses its flagellum as a kind of oar to move itself around.

What are euglenas?

Euglenas are one of the strangest kinds of protists. Euglenas can make food using sunlight, as plants can. But in other ways they are not like plants at all. Euglenas can move around, using a long, whiplike projection called a **flagellum** that they beat backward and forward.

Amebas

Amebas are single-celled protists. Giant amebas are just big enough for you to see without a microscope. An ameba takes in its food by wrapping itself around it. The ameba then absorbs the food through its outer cell membrane.

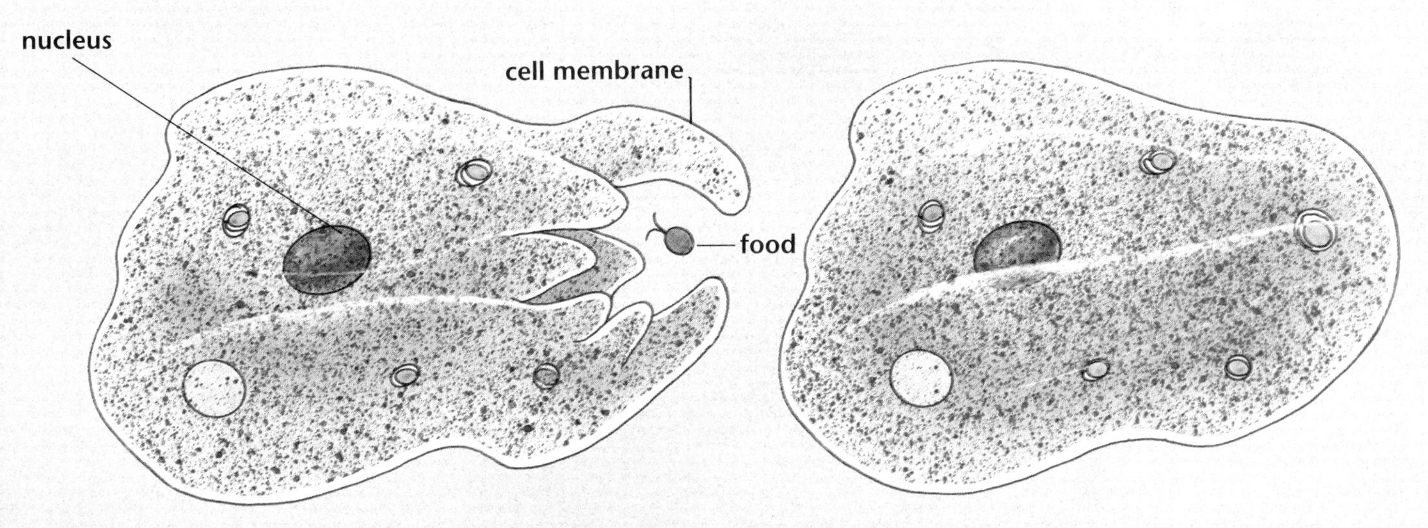

A single-celled ameba moves around in the water until it finds food. Part of the ameba's body surrounds the food, which is then absorbed through the membrane.

The food floats inside the ameba's body until it is absorbed. Then any waste can pass out through the membrane.

How does an ameba move?

You can use the model cell described on pages 18 and 19 to show how an ameba moves.

1. Hold the model steady with one hand and pull one side of the plastic bag out with your other hand.

2. Now squeeze the gelatin into the part of the bag you have pulled out.

3. Repeat this several times, and you will see that your model has moved forward a little way.

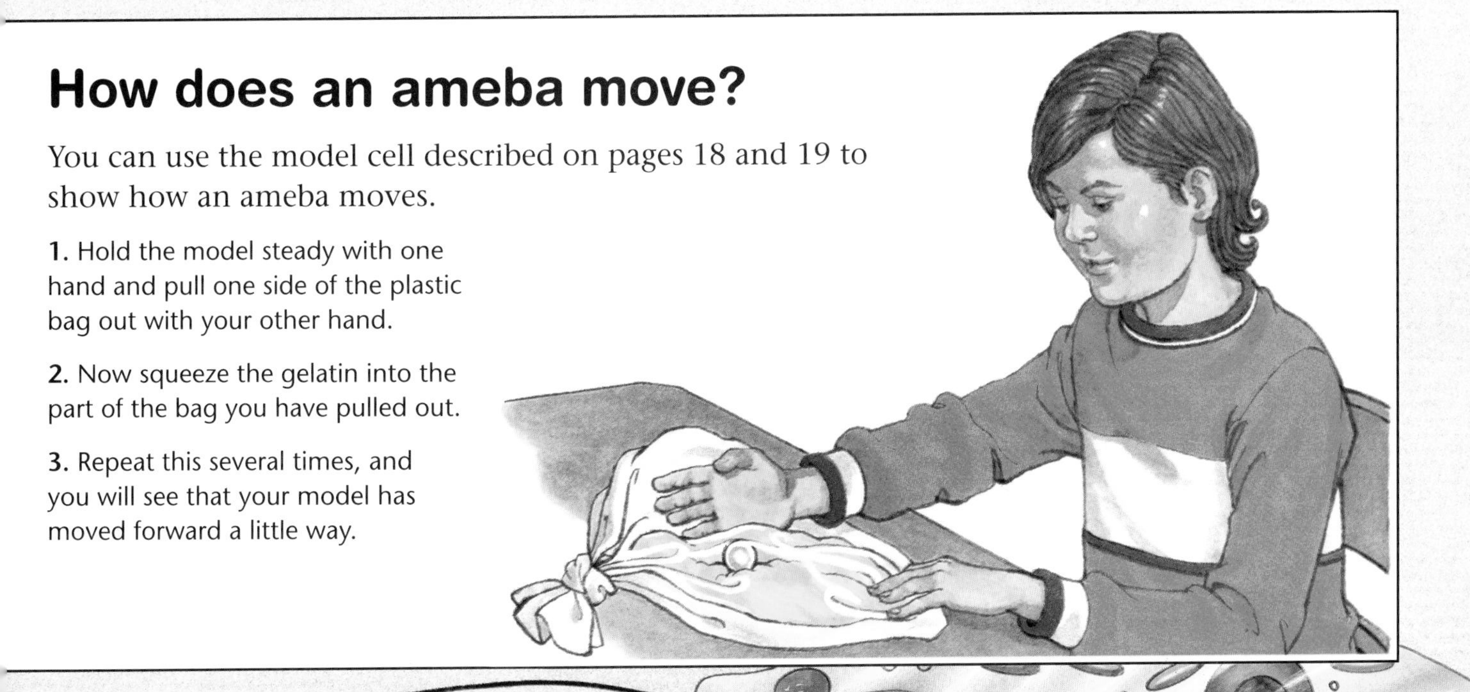

What are algae?

Algae are simple organisms that live mostly in water. Some algae live on land, growing on certain plants or living on sloths or turtles. Other algae may grow within animals or plants. Scientists classify blue-green algae as prokaryotes. All other algae are protists.

Many algae live in the surface layers of the water in seas and lakes. Together with minute animals they form a group of living things called **plankton.** Some algae attach themselves to surfaces, such as rocks, and stay in one place all their life. Other kinds of algae drift about in the water. Many algae make their own food by photosynthesis.

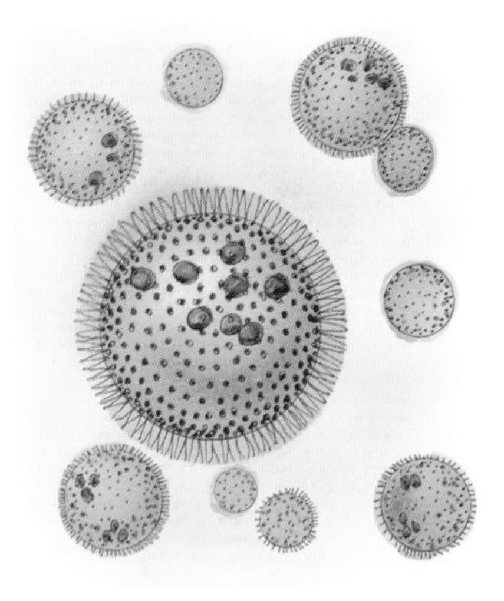

Volvox is a green alga that grows in colonies. The colonies are round and consist of many cells.

Simple organisms

Chlorococcum is a single-celled alga that lives on trees and damp walls. Chlamydomonas is a single-celled alga that swims about in water.

Some algae live together in groups called **colonies.** Volvox is an alga that lives in colonies and moves about freely. Spirogyra is an alga that does not move about at all.

Swimming algae

You will need:

aluminum foil

green pond water (as green as possible)

clean water (allowed to sit for 24 hours, to allow the chlorine to evaporate)

scissors

a small glass jar

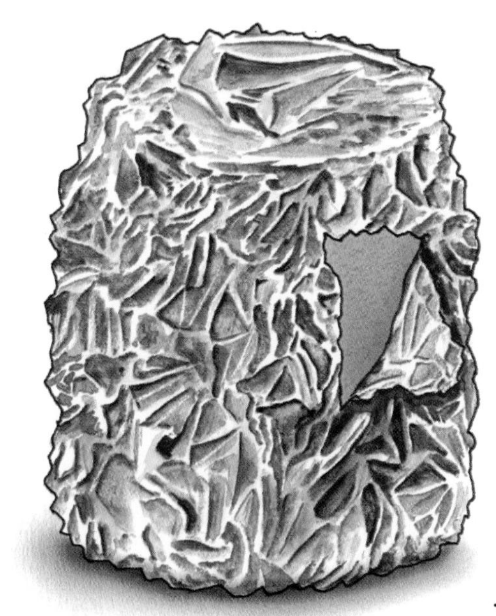

1. Ask an adult to help you collect some green pond water in a glass jar. Pour in some of the clean water. Wash your hands afterward, because the pond water can make you ill.

2. Cover the jar completely with aluminum foil, and then cut a small hole in one side of the cover. Stand the jar on a window sill with the hole facing the window.

3. Carefully lift the cover after an hour or two. What has happened? Do you know why?

You'll find the green water clustered around the spot where the hole was. The tiny algae that make the water green have swum toward the light.

Find out more by looking at pages **84–85**

Seaweed grows underwater and on rocky shores.

Seaweeds

Seaweeds are also algae. Seaweeds grow in many different shapes, sizes, and colors. Red and brown seaweeds contain some of the green chlorophyll needed for photosynthesis. Such organisms can't survive in the darkness of deep water, so seaweeds and other algae grow only in shallow water.

In the middle of the Atlantic Ocean, there are large floating patches of a seaweed called sargassum. The place where the sargassum grows is called the Sargasso Sea. The patches of sargassum may be some 100 feet (30 meters) in diameter. Sometimes a mass of the weed can cover more than 1 acre (0.4 hectare).

Tasty seaweeds

Have you ever eaten seaweed? Many seaweeds, such as wakame, dulse, kombu, and arame, can be eaten as vegetables or in soups. Some seaweeds produce a jelly called agar, which is used to make ice cream!

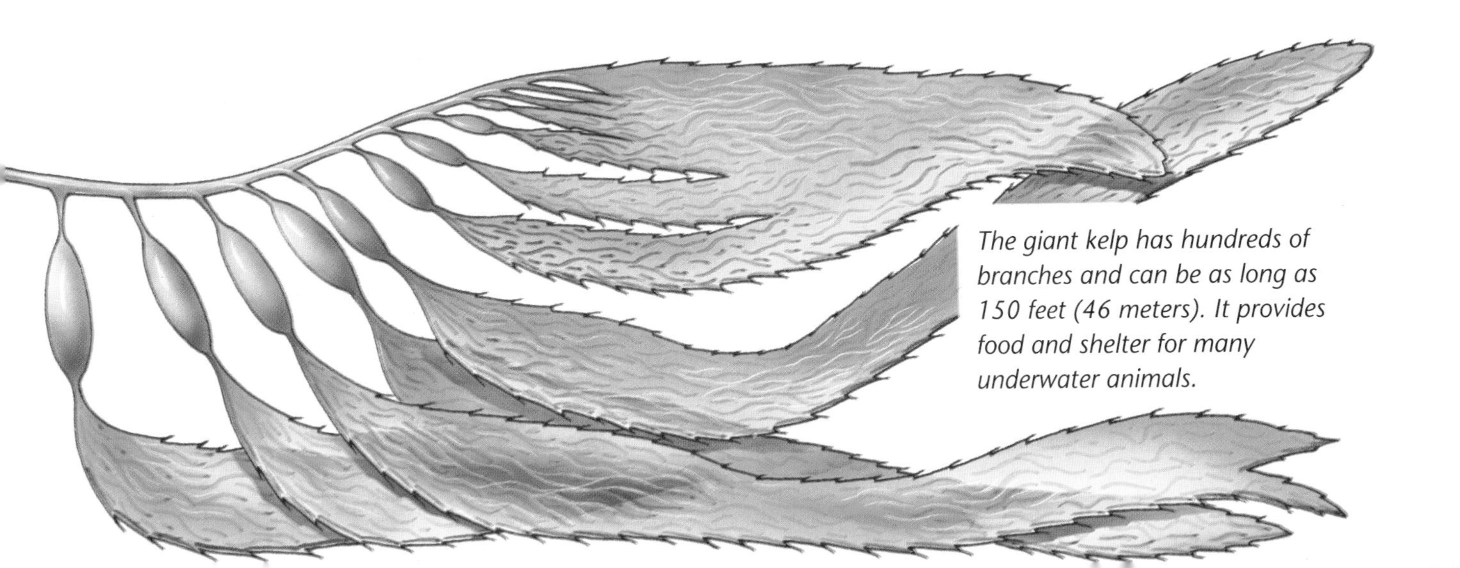

The giant kelp has hundreds of branches and can be as long as 150 feet (46 meters). It provides food and shelter for many underwater animals.

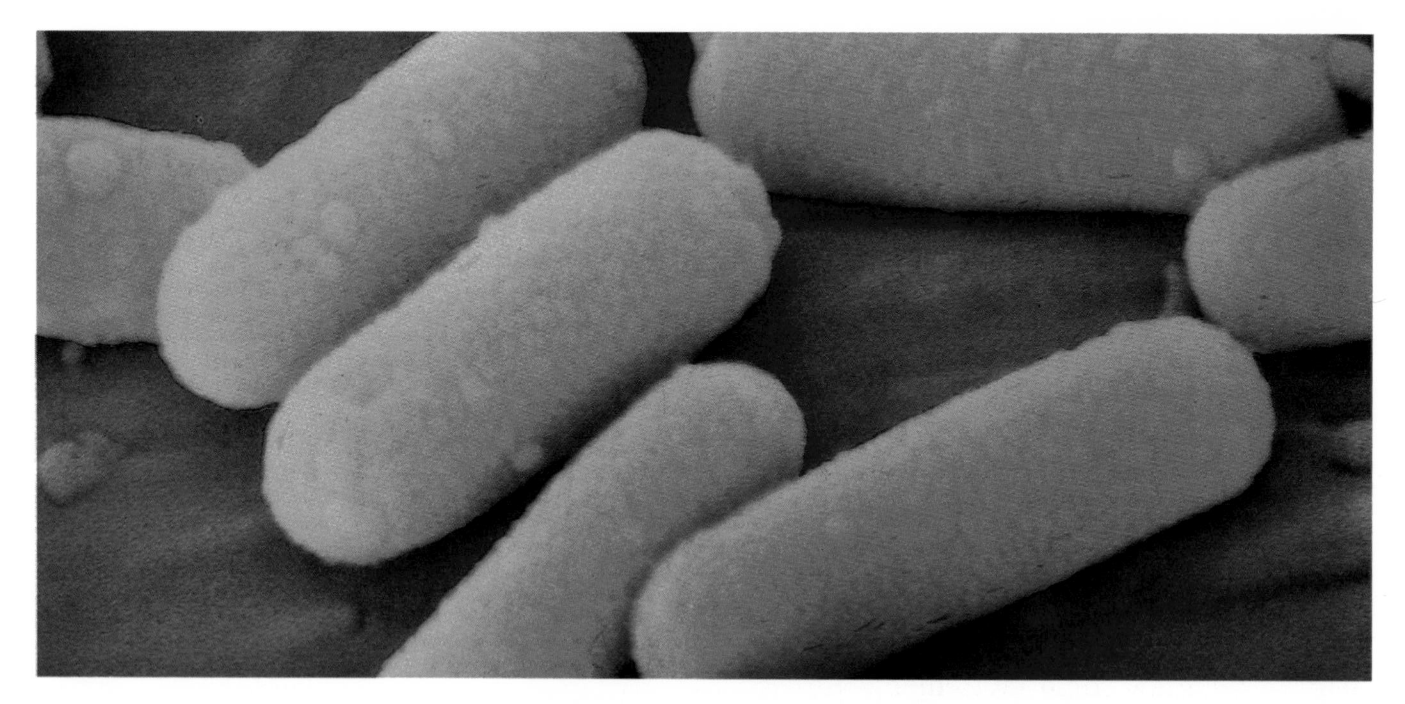

These rod-shaped bacteria are on the head of a pin. The photograph is enlarged many times.

What are bacteria?

Bacteria are very small living things that have only one cell. Some kinds of bacteria can make their own food from sunlight, like green plants do. But there are many differences between plants and bacteria. So scientists say that bacteria belong to a separate kingdom of living things, which is called the **prokaryote** kingdom. There are thousands of different kinds of bacteria. Each bacterium is so small that you need a powerful microscope to see it.

Where do bacteria live?

Some kinds of bacteria live on you! There are millions of bacteria on your skin and inside your mouth, nose, and lungs. A great many live in your intestines. Other kinds of bacteria live in the air, in water, or in the top layers of soil.

Harmful bacteria

Bacteria can be spherical, rod-shaped, or spiral. Each of these harmful bacteria causes a serious illness or disease.

Spherical bacteria

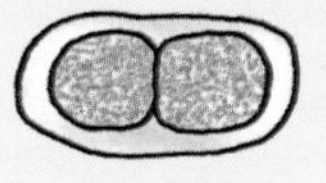

pneumonia

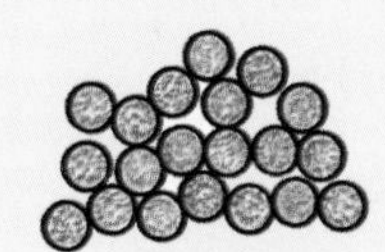

boils
blood poisoning

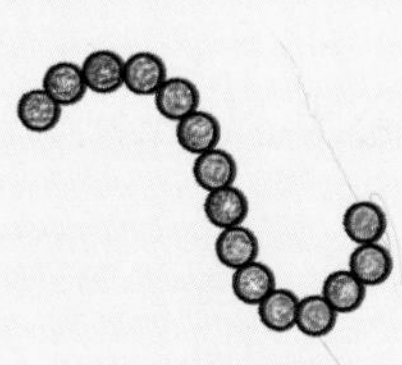

sore throat
scarlet fever

Find out more by looking at pages **18–19**
20–21
32–33

What do bacteria do?

Many kinds of bacteria are useful. They help living things to survive and be healthy. Some of the bacteria on your skin protect you from other tiny living things that might harm you. Those in your intestines help break down the waste products that your body eliminates. They even help to make vitamins that keep you healthy. We use bacteria to make some types of cheese and yogurt.

Bacteria in soil and water help break down animal droppings and the dead bodies of animals and plants. These all contain chemical elements, such as carbon and nitrogen. Some bacteria help change these chemical elements into other substances. These substances can then be used again by other living things.

But not all bacteria are helpful. Some kinds of bacteria destroy healthy cells and cause diseases. Whooping cough and food poisoning are caused by bacteria. Animals and plants suffer illnesses, too. Anthrax, a cattle disease, is caused by bacteria. Bacteria also cause certain kinds of rot and blight in plants.

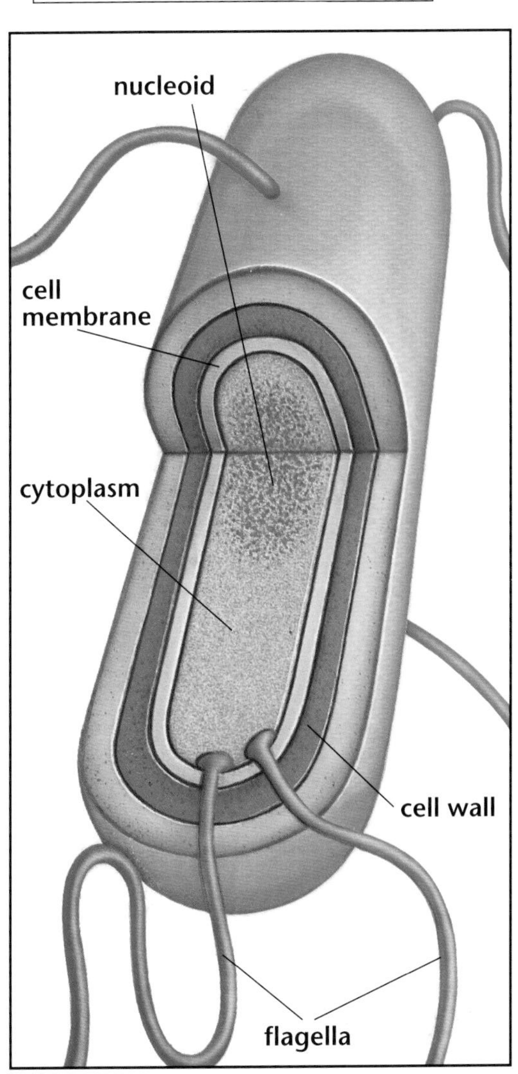

In this rod-shaped bacteria, the cell wall and cell membrane surround and protect the cytoplasm, which contains the cell's nucleoid.

How do bacteria take in food?

Bacteria are surrounded by a thick cell membrane with no openings to take in solid food. Some bacteria contain chlorophyll, which can make food with the help of sunlight. Others soak up fluids from the body in which they live.

Bacteria that live on rotting plants or animals use chemical proteins called enzymes. These can turn the dead matter into simpler liquids. The bacteria then soak up the liquid through their cell membrane.

Rod-shaped bacteria

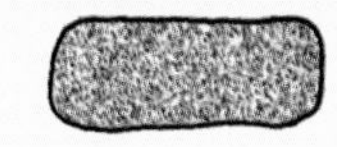

tuberculosis

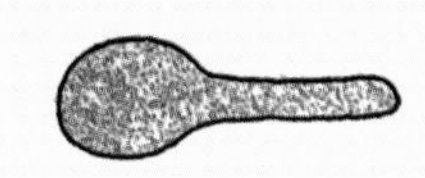

tetanus

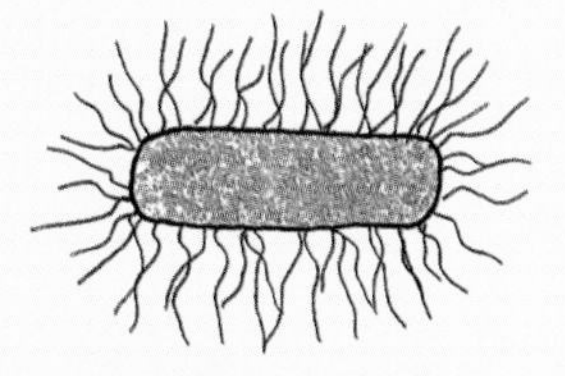

typhoid fever

Spiral bacterium

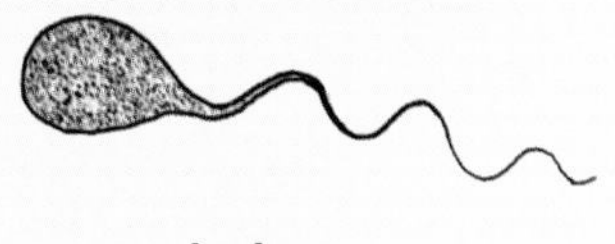

cholera

Some fungi are extremely poisonous! Never touch or eat wild fungi without asking an adult first.

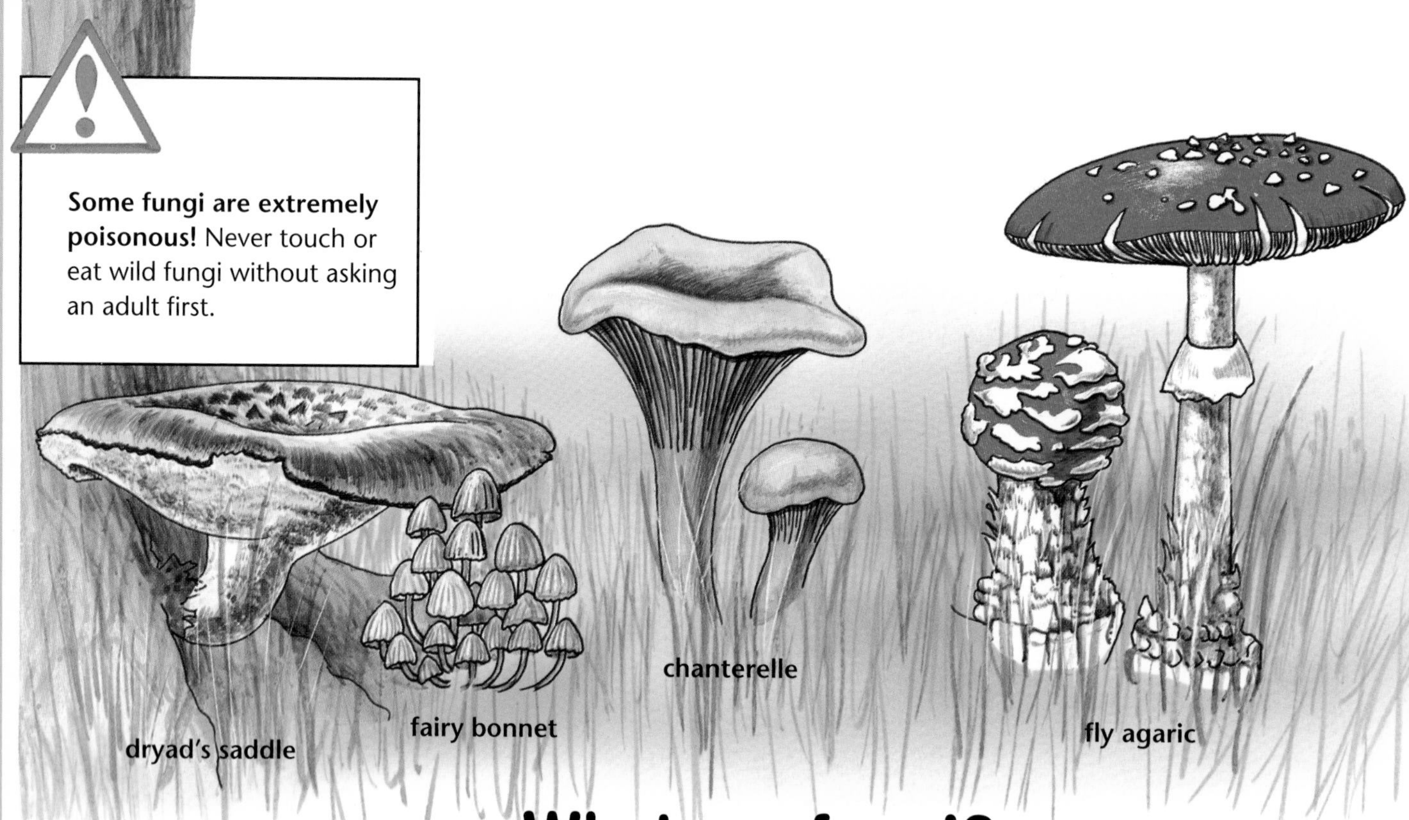

What are fungi?

Do you like eating fungi? It doesn't sound very good to eat, does it? Mold and mushrooms are both kinds of fungus. Certain kinds of mushrooms are good to eat. But most kinds of mushrooms and toadstools and nearly all other kinds of fungus are not good to eat. Some are deadly poisonous, so don't be tempted to taste them.

Botanists have named at least 70,000 kinds, or species, of fungus. And there are many more to discover! Some fungi are easy to see because the parts that produce the spores are large. These fungi include mushrooms, toadstools, puffballs, and bracket fungi, which look like shelves sticking out of a tree trunk.

Fungi can be many different colors but not green. That's because fungi do not contain chlorophyll, which is the green chemical found in many plants.

Different fungal molds are growing on this cake. A mold grows from a tiny spore that settles on damp food. The mold produces capsules containing thousands of spores.

Where do fungi get their food?

Fungi like to grow where it's dark and damp. Most fungi feed off dead and rotting plants. Some fungi are **parasites**, which means they get their food from living plants or animals. Many crops can be damaged or even killed by these fungi.

Find out more by looking at pages **84–85**

Fairy rings

Have you ever seen a **fairy ring?** A fairy ring is a small group of mushrooms growing in a circle in a field or on a lawn. The fairy ring has lots of separate mushrooms above ground, but it's all part of the same growth. Underground, lots of thin threads absorb food from the soil. Except for some one-celled fungi, most other fungi have these thin threads, called **hyphae**, which take in food from living or decaying things.

New fungi grow from spores. Mushroom spores grow in the thin walls called **gills** on the underside of the umbrella-shaped cap. Puffball spores form inside a baglike structure. If a raindrop falls on a puffball, a little cloud of spores puffs out.

Old man's beard is an unusual lichen that hangs from tree branches. It grows up to 5 feet (1.5 meters) long.

What are lichens?

Have you ever noticed crusty gray-green patches growing on old walls or trees or rocks? These are called lichens. Lichens are organisms that consist of fungi and algae living together. The fungi make use of the food that the algae provide, and the algae use the protection provided by the fungi.

Lichens have no leaves, stems, or roots. They grow very slowly and can live for thousands of years. Lichens are also very hardy. They can survive the coldest weather and the harshest winds. If you traveled as far south as possible, or as far north as possible, lichens would be the last growing things you saw before you reached the North and South poles. Most lichens are sensitive to air pollution, so the greatest variety can be found where the air is cleanest.

Botanists divide lichens into three groups. **Crustose**, or crustlike, lichens lie flat on the surface where they grow. **Foliose**, or leaflike, lichens are flat, rounded, leaf-shaped lichens of many different colors. **Fruticose**, or shrublike, lichens look like tiny bushes with long, hairy stems.

Arctic lichens cover much of the ground surface in the tundra. They provide food for caribou and reindeer.

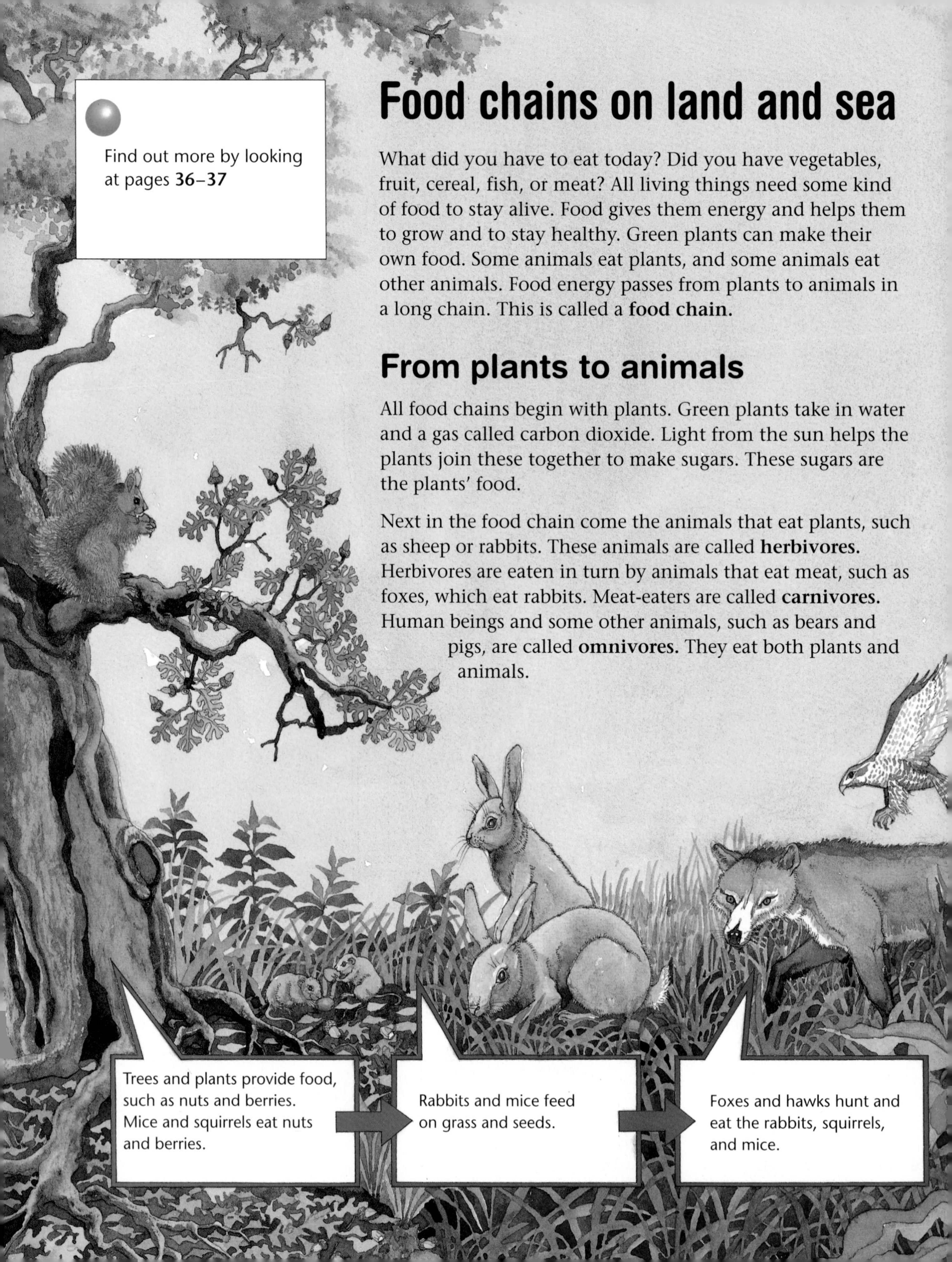

Find out more by looking at pages **36–37**

Food chains on land and sea

What did you have to eat today? Did you have vegetables, fruit, cereal, fish, or meat? All living things need some kind of food to stay alive. Food gives them energy and helps them to grow and to stay healthy. Green plants can make their own food. Some animals eat plants, and some animals eat other animals. Food energy passes from plants to animals in a long chain. This is called a **food chain.**

From plants to animals

All food chains begin with plants. Green plants take in water and a gas called carbon dioxide. Light from the sun helps the plants join these together to make sugars. These sugars are the plants' food.

Next in the food chain come the animals that eat plants, such as sheep or rabbits. These animals are called **herbivores.** Herbivores are eaten in turn by animals that eat meat, such as foxes, which eat rabbits. Meat-eaters are called **carnivores.** Human beings and some other animals, such as bears and pigs, are called **omnivores.** They eat both plants and animals.

Trees and plants provide food, such as nuts and berries. Mice and squirrels eat nuts and berries.

Rabbits and mice feed on grass and seeds.

Foxes and hawks hunt and eat the rabbits, squirrels, and mice.

More herbivores than carnivores

The grasslands of Africa are covered in grasses and other plants. Between periodic droughts, there is usually plenty of sunlight, carbon dioxide, and water for these plants to grow and make their own food. Herds of antelopes feed on the plants. But a herbivore such as an antelope stores only about 10 to 20 percent of the energy from its food. About 80 to 90 percent of the energy is used by the antelope to carry out life functions.

This pyramid shape gives an idea of the proportion of living things in each link of a food chain in the grasslands of Africa. At the top of the pyramid, there are few carnivores. Lower down, there are more herbivores, which feed the carnivores. At the base of the pyramid, there are even more plants, which feed the herbivores.

Small groups of lions prey on the antelopes. When a carnivore such as a lion eats a herbivore such as an antelope, the carnivore gets only the 10 to 20 percent of energy stored in the body of the herbivore. The farther along the food chain you go, the less stored energy there is available. This means there must be many more antelopes than lions. Similarly, there must be many, many plants to support the antelope population.

Food chains in the sea

There are plants in the lakes and ocean as well as on land. Tiny plants and animals are part of a layer of millions of living things near the surface of the ocean. All these things are called **plankton**. The plankton that are plants use light from the sun to help make their own food. The plankton that are animals eat the plants or each other.

Fish, shellfish, and seabirds feed on the plankton. Then these creatures are eaten by larger animals, such as seals and some types of whales. This makes a food chain in the sea. So the food chains of the sea begin with plankton.

Do you sometimes eat fish? If you do, then you are at the end of a food chain.

Return to the soil

Find out more by looking at pages **26–27**
30–31
34–35

Most food in the world initially comes from plants. Plants provide food for animals. The animals are then eaten by other animals that are in a food chain. So, animal life depends on plants.

Green plants use carbon dioxide, water, and sunlight to make their food. Plants also soak up substances called **nutrients** from the soil, which make them grow. Nutrients include chemicals that contain nitrogen, which plants and animals need. When an animal eats a plant, the nutrients in the plant pass into its body. If that animal is then eaten by another animal, the nutrients will be passed on again.

After the nutrients have been used by plants and animals, they return to the soil to help more plants to grow. The nutrients return to the soil through animal droppings and through dead plants and animals that decay in the ground.

Bacteria at work

What makes dead plants and animals decay? They decay because millions of tiny bacteria feed on them. You may have seen a rotten apple or the remains of a dead animal lying along the roadside. In time, bacteria will eat away at them and break them down into smaller and simpler pieces. In this way, bacteria break down dead plants and animals until they become part of the soil.

Bacteria use only a certain amount of the nutrients from the dead plants and animals that they eat. They return the rest of the nutrients to the soil. This is how the soil is provided with a fresh supply of nutrients.

Bacteria feed on the flesh of this damaged fruit. The bacteria eat away at the apple until it breaks down into the soil.

Energy from the sun passes, in the form of food, from one living thing to another.

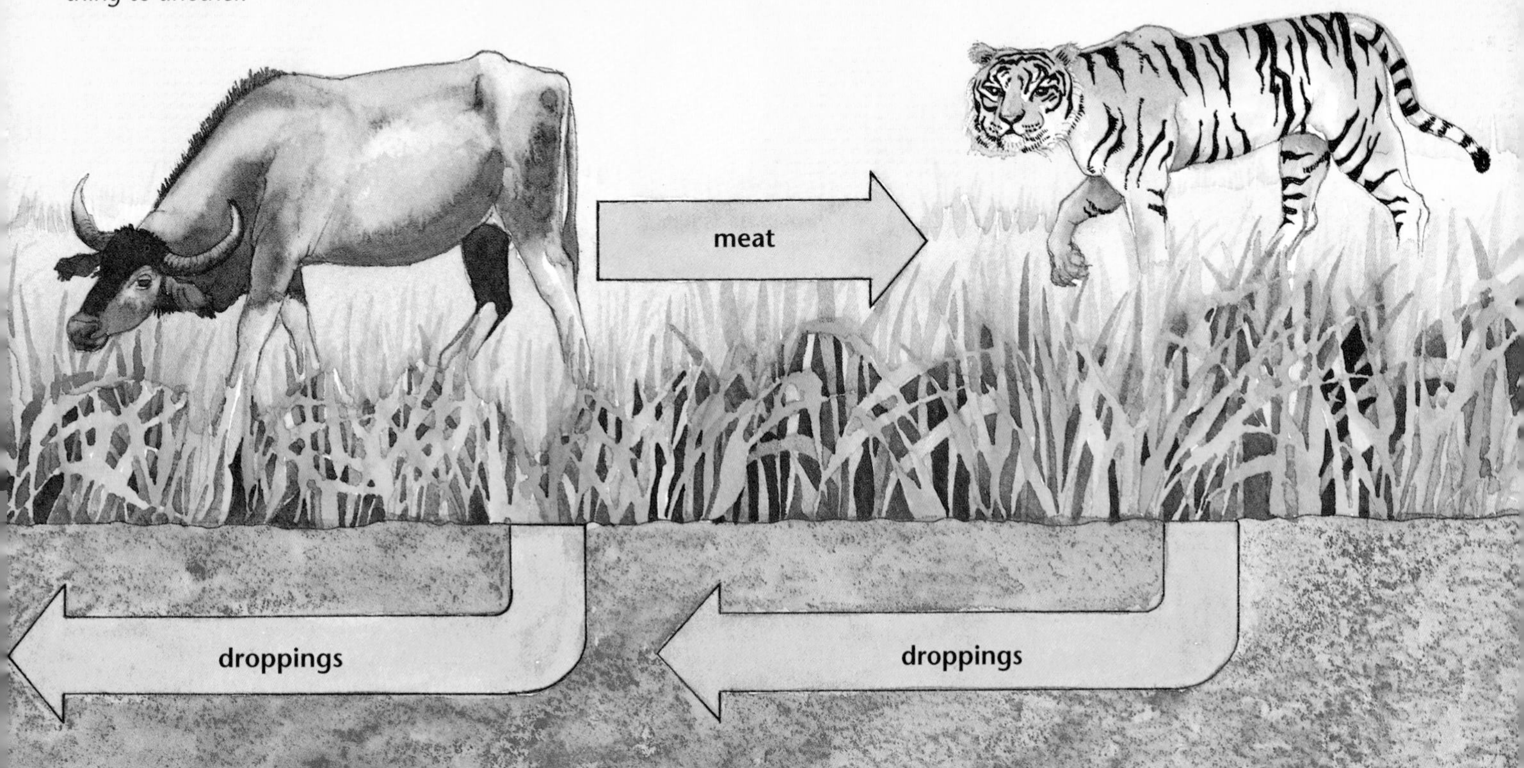

These fungi are growing on a rotting tree trunk. They help to break down the wood into small pieces.

What happens in the soil?

Have you ever seen toadstools growing on dead trees? Or a greenish mold on an old piece of bread? If you have, then you have seen **fungi** growing. Both toadstools and molds are fungi. Fungi help to break down dead plants and animals into smaller and simpler pieces. This is part of the process of decay that happens to dead things. When dead things decay, they are said to be **decomposing.** Living things that make dead plants and animals decay are called **decomposers**.

Fungi are important decomposers. Some fungi are so small that you can't see them without a microscope. These tiny fungi, along with bacteria, do most of the work in breaking down dead plants and animals and other waste.

Find out more by looking at pages **32–33**

Animal decomposers

Some animals help to decompose dead things. Many ants grow fungi on dead leaves for food. Dung beetles eat animal droppings, which are sometimes called dung. Other insects, such as woodlice and springtails, feed on decaying plants and meat.

Dung beetles lay their eggs in animal droppings. When the eggs hatch, the young feed on the dung. Woodlice and springtails feed mostly on rotting plants.

springtail

What is humus?

When dead plants and animals in the ground have completely decayed, they form a dark-brown substance—called **humus**—in the soil. Humus holds water in the soil and provides the nutrients that plants need to grow.

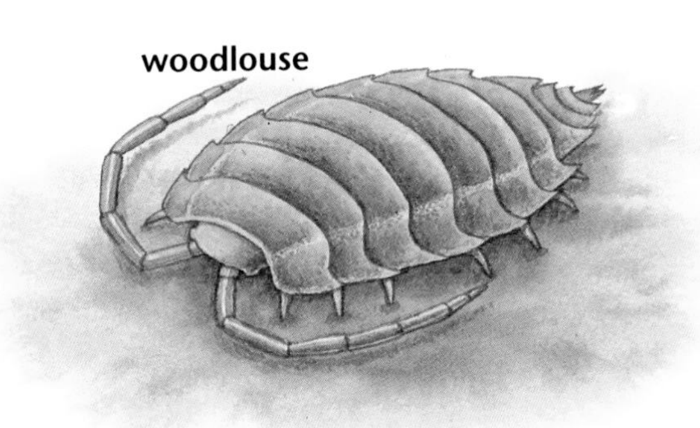

So decomposers have an important job to do. Without them there would be no humus or nutrients in the soil, and plants could not grow. The animals would die because there would be no food for them. The decomposers are a special group of living things that keep life going on and on.

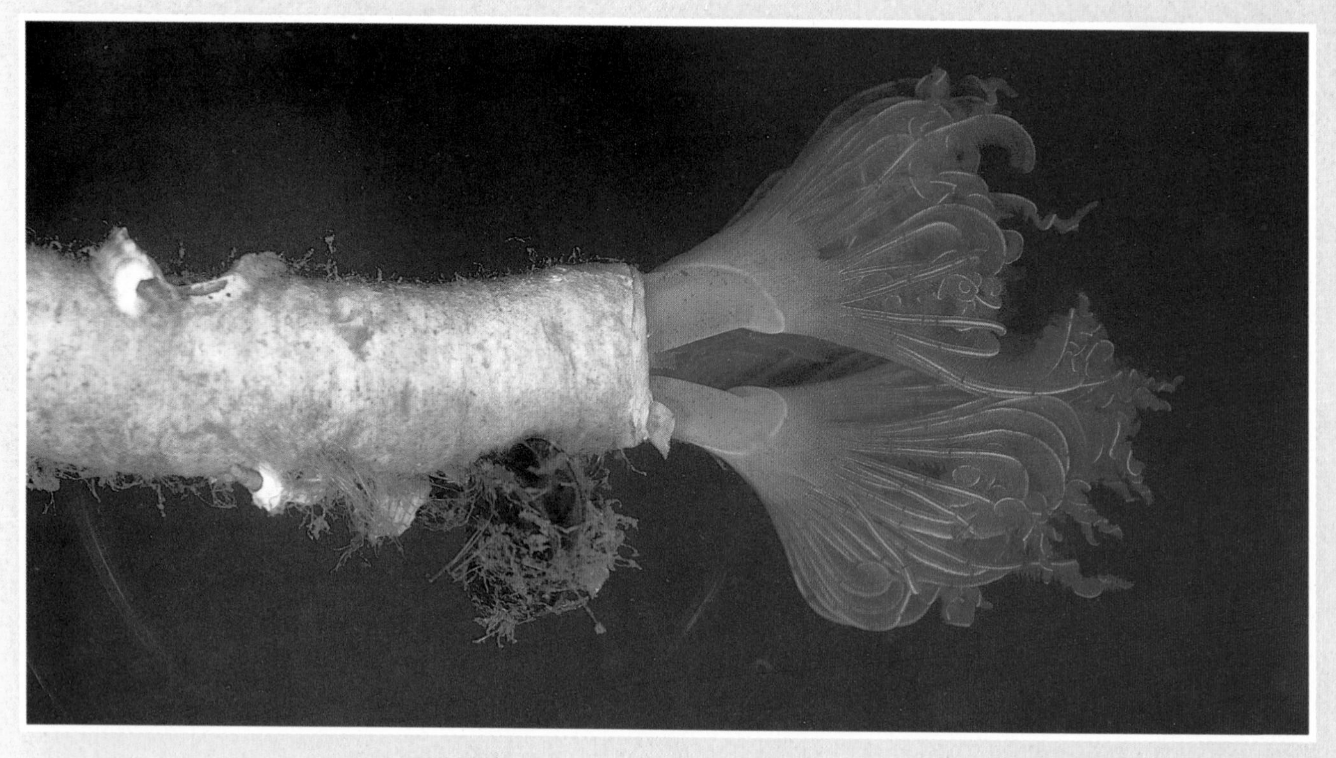

A fanworm catches food particles by waving its feathery tentacles in the water.

How do living things eat?

Eating is easy! Most animals take food in at one end of their body. The food is squeezed through a long tube inside them, and the waste passes out at the other end of the body.

Many animals chew their food before it goes down into their stomach. Have you ever noticed a cow eating? Its jaws move around and around, grinding its food. Carnivores, such as tigers, have sharp teeth that tear their food with an up-and-down movement. Some animals don't chew their food at all. Many birds swallow fish or grain whole.

Pelicans use their pouch to scoop fish out of the water. Then they swallow the fish whole.

Different ways of eating

Other living things eat in very different ways. The starfish has a special way of taking food into its stomach. Its mouth is in the middle of its body. When the starfish is about to eat, it pushes its stomach through its mouth. Still attached to the starfish's mouth, the stomach surrounds the food and digests it slowly, before returning to the body through the mouth. Waste food is passed back out through the mouth.

Barnacles fasten themselves to rocks and other objects in the sea. They feed by sweeping their feathery tentacles through the water. They are called **filter feeders** because they use their tentacles like a sieve to pick up tiny particles of food floating close by. Many other sea animals, from simple sponges to the giant blue whale, are filter feeders.

Unlike most animals, termites can eat dry, dead wood. They can digest the wood because they have special bacteria in their intestines.

Earthworms feed on tiny particles of dead plants in the soil. As they move along, earthworms swallow the soil and digest the particles of dead and decaying plants. The rest of the soil passes through their body and is left behind as waste.

An aphid feeds on plant juices. It has a mouth shaped like a tube, which can pierce the plant stems or leaves. Aphids suck the plant juices in somewhat the same way that people suck a drink through a drinking straw.

How do green plants eat?

Green plants make their own food by a process called **photosynthesis.** They use light from the sun, a gas called carbon dioxide from the air, and water from the soil. Using the energy from the sun to mix these ingredients, plants make sugars that they use as food.

Find out more by looking at pages **20–21**
38–39

Aphids pierce the leaves of plants with their sharp mouth. Then they suck up the plant juices.

Find out more by looking at pages **36–37**
40–41

Using food

What happens to food once it's inside an animal's body? Food contains many different substances, such as **proteins** and **carbohydrates**, that living creatures need. Carbohydrates are needed to provide energy. Proteins are needed to help animals grow and stay healthy. The food has to be broken down into lots of smaller, simpler substances, so that the body can absorb them. This process is called **digestion**.

Juices at work

Digestion begins in the mouth when an animal chews its food. A digestive juice called **saliva** and a chemical substance called an **enzyme** start breaking down the food. When the food reaches the stomach, it's broken down some more by acid. Here, more enzymes further break down the food.

After the acid and enzymes break down the food in the stomach, the food is slowly pushed along into a tube called the **small intestine**. Here, several more enzymes help to complete, for the most part, the process of digestion. Important parts of the food—the nutrients—are absorbed into the blood vessels that line the wall of the small intestine. Inside the bloodstream, the nutrients are pumped around the body.

The stomach of a cow or a sheep has four sections. The grass that the animal eats is chewed and broken down more than once before it reaches the intestine.

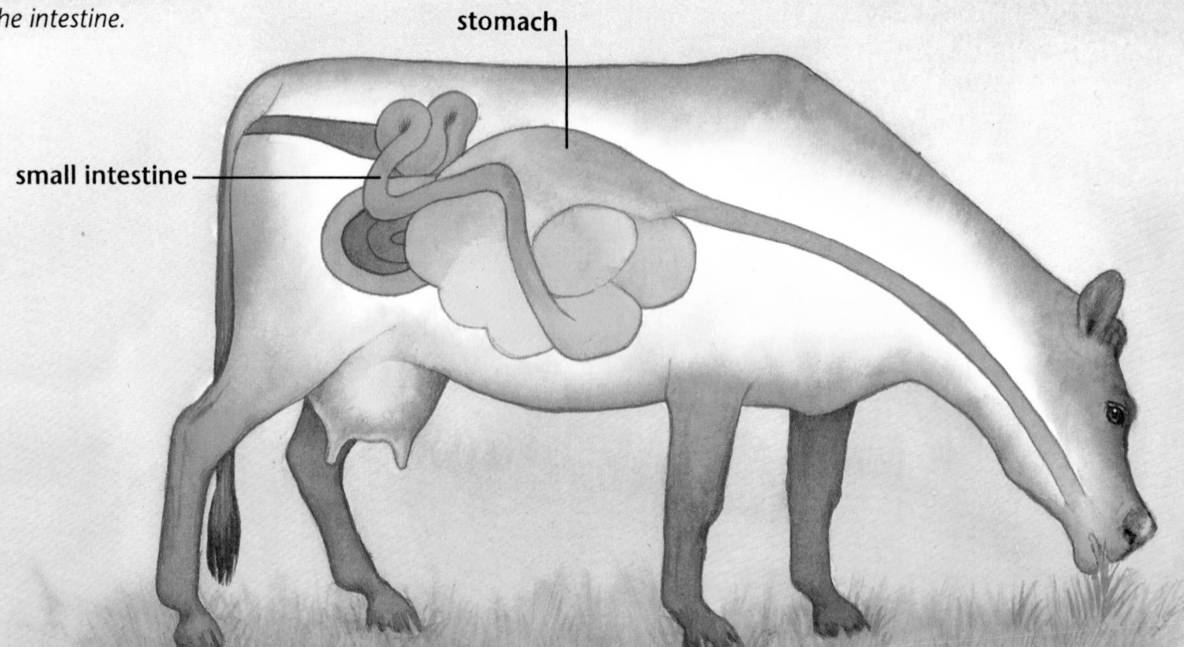

A special stomach

Some plant-eaters, such as goats and cows, have an interesting digestive system. They have a stomach with four separate sections. When the animal swallows a mouthful of grass, it is collected in the first and second sections. In the second section, the grass is softened into **cud.** As the animal rests, stomach muscles return the cud to its mouth where it is chewed again and mixed with saliva. After the second chewing, the food goes through all the sections of the stomach to the intestine.

Some spiders digest their food outside their body. They do this by injecting digestive juices into the insects they catch. After a while, the digestive juices break down the insides of the insects into a digestible fluid. Then the spiders suck in this fluid from the insects. Houseflies digest their food by squirting saliva over their food and sucking up the liquid that results.

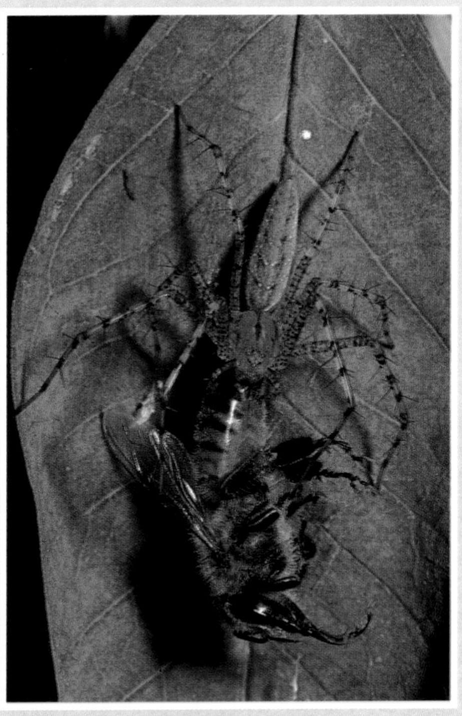

The lynx spider's prey is often much larger than itself. The spider injects enzymes into the victim's body. The enzymes are chemicals that turn the insides of the body to a juice that the spider can digest.

Why do animals need food?

Animals need food as a source of energy. Energy is what keeps body parts moving and working properly. Food is also used as material to make bodies grow and to repair parts that have become impaired or worn out. After the food is digested, the body uses the chemicals from the broken-down food to build up the body. Animals can also store some types of food as **fat** inside their body. It is used whenever it is needed, usually for energy.

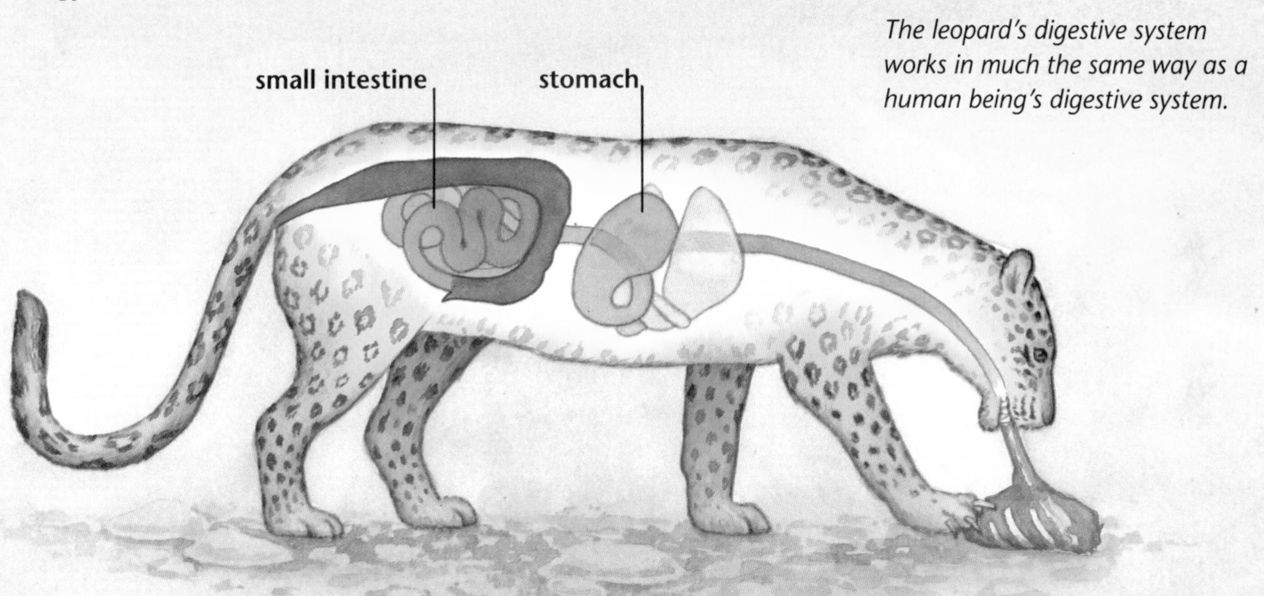

The leopard's digestive system works in much the same way as a human being's digestive system.

Find out more by looking
at pages **38–39**
42–43

Getting rid of waste

Food keeps living things alive. But animals cannot use all the food they eat. As food passes through the body, only some of it is digested. The body takes in all the parts of the food that it needs and then gets rid of the rest. In most animals, waste food is sent through the lower part of the body and finally comes out of the opening called the **anus.** This solid waste food that comes out of the bodies of humans and other animals is called **feces.**

In addition to solid waste food, animals need to get rid of other substances that are harmful to them. In vertebrates, this job is done by the **kidneys.** The kidneys collect all the unwanted chemicals and excess water and turn them into a liquid called **urine.** The urine is then stored in another part of the body, called the **bladder**, until it leaves the body.

Most birds produce feces and liquid waste together and release the waste through the anus. Their droppings are feces in the middle with a coat of thick, white liquid waste on the outside. Other kinds of animals, such as reptiles and insects, also release their waste through the anus. Some simple animals don't have a special opening for waste. Their waste products have to go out through the mouth or through some part of the body wall.

Mammals release carbon dioxide, urine, and feces from their body. If for any reason an animal is not able to get rid of this waste, it will become ill.

Plant waste

Even plants clear out the things they don't need. Some mangrove trees, for example, have too much salt in them because they grow in salty places. They get rid of the salt by pumping it into special leaves. These leaves then fall from the tree.

Mangrove trees can get rid of waste salt by storing it in special leaves. These leaves fall from the tree, taking the waste with them.

Other types of waste

What else do animals take into their bodies, use, and then send out as waste? The answer is gases. We all breathe in a gas called **oxygen** from the air. Oxygen helps the food inside our body break down, in order to release energy. This energy production inside us makes a waste gas called **carbon dioxide.** We get rid of this by breathing it out into the air.

Breathing

We need to breathe to stay alive. **Breathing** is a process of taking in and releasing certain gases, chiefly oxygen and carbon dioxide. Almost all living things need to breathe to survive.

When an animal **inhales** (breathes in), it takes in oxygen, which then enters its blood and is transported to every cell in its body. The food it eats contains sugars that are also transported to every cell in the body. These sugars are split up in each cell by chemicals called enzymes, and energy is released. Oxygen is essential to this process of splitting up sugars and other foods and of releasing the energy stored within them.

When a cell releases energy from food, a gas called carbon dioxide is released. This gas enters the blood and is **exhaled** (breathed out) at the same place as oxygen is inhaled.

How different kinds of animals breathe

Mammals, birds, and reptiles breathe by inhaling air into parts of their bodies called lungs. **Lungs** are like stretchy bags that become larger as air flows in. They become smaller as air and carbon dioxide are exhaled. Breathing is rhythmical and automatic.

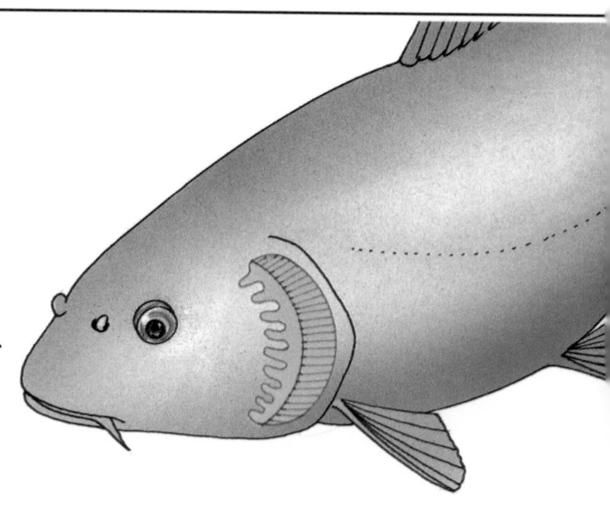

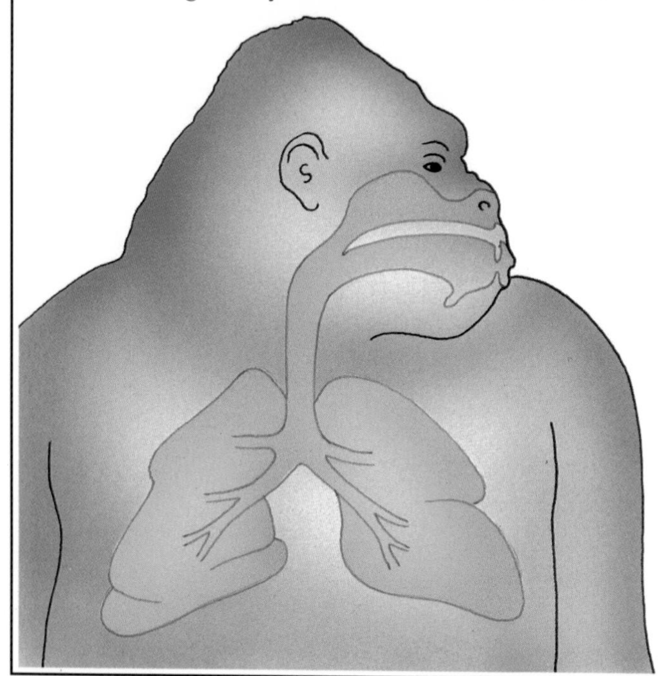

Fish and many other water animals take in water and pass it through body parts called **gills.** Gills absorb the oxygen that is dissolved in the water.

Mudskippers are fish that come onto land to feed. They are able to do this because they have **sacs** (baglike structures), in their mouth and gill cavities. These sacs are richly supplied with blood, which enables the mudskipper to absorb oxygen directly from the air.

Plants breathe, too!

Even plants need to take in oxygen from the air. The oxygen helps a plant's cells to release energy from sugars that are stored inside the plant. Plants give out a small amount of carbon dioxide, especially during the night.

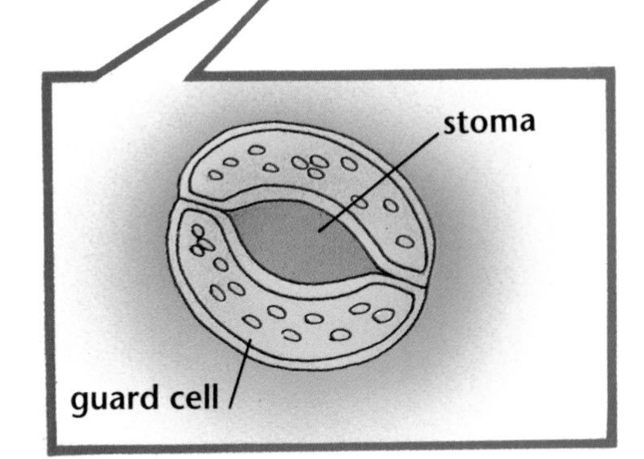

During the day, when plants make their food, they do the opposite. They take in carbon dioxide from the air and give out oxygen. They do this in sunlight by photosynthesis. The oxygen and carbon dioxide pass in and out of the leaf through tiny holes called **stomata.** Each stoma has two guard cells that help it open and close. Plants give out oxygen, which animals breathe in, and animals breathe out carbon dioxide, which plants take in.

Insects breathe through a network of tubes. These tubes reach every part of the insect's body.

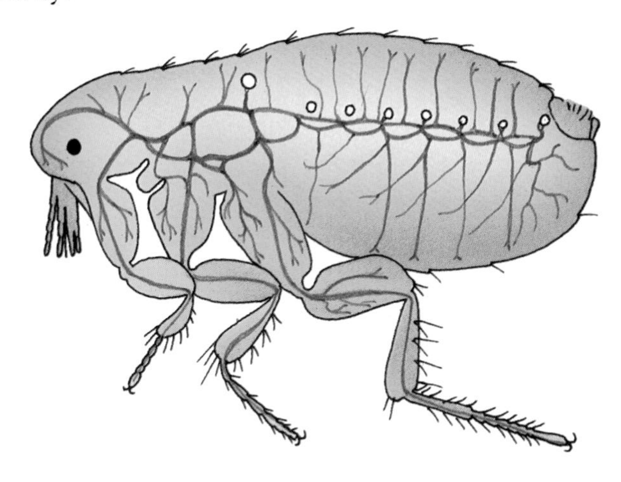

Water spiders breathe air directly, so this spider takes its own air bubble down into the water.

Energy for living

Do you like to play games that make you run very fast or jump in the air? You need a lot of energy to do these things. Energy is what our muscles use to move our bodies. Every time you walk, ride a bicycle, or move in any way, your muscles are using up energy. Without energy, your heart would stop beating and you would soon die. So people also need energy to make the internal parts of their body function. In the same way, all living things need energy so that their bodies can stay alive and work properly.

Different animals have very different energy needs. This chart shows the amount of food each creature eats in a week compared with its body weight.

puma—97 pounds (44 kilograms)

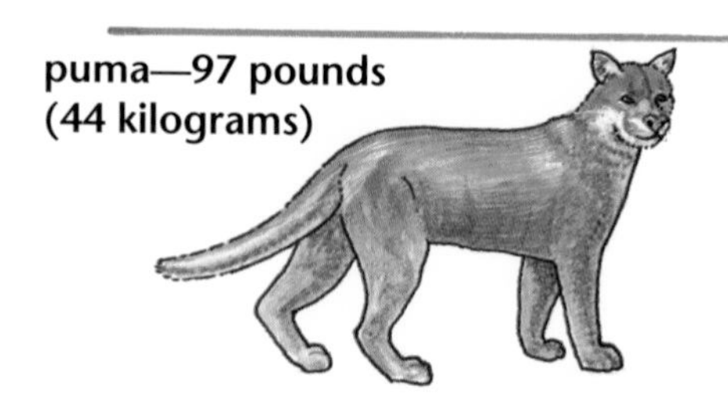

A puma eats about 7.7 pounds (3.5 kilograms) of food each day. That's 8 percent of its body weight.

54 pounds (24.5 kilograms) in a week

locust—0.035 ounce (1 gram)

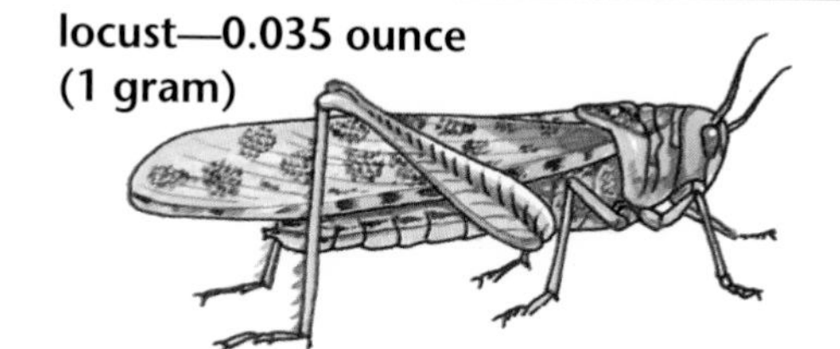

A locust eats about 0.02 ounce (0.5 gram) of food every day. That's 50 percent of its body weight.

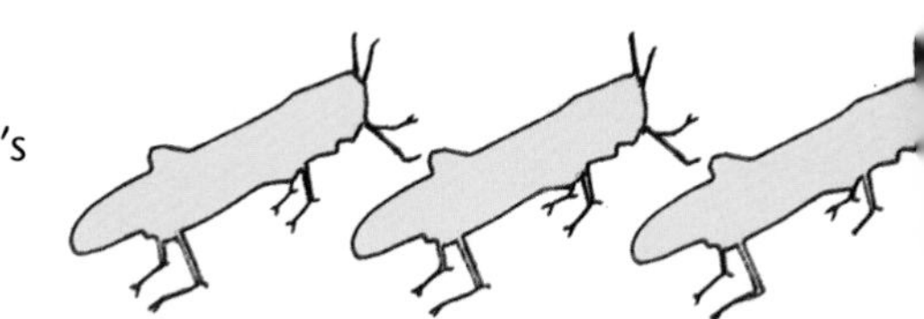

penguin—88 pounds (40 kilograms)

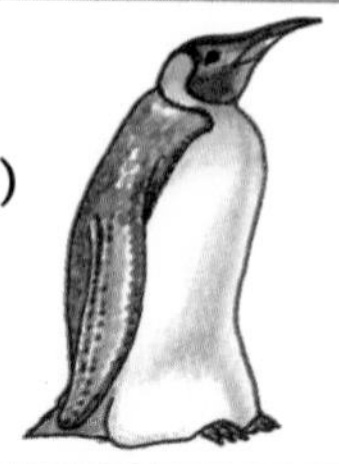

A penguin eats up to 176 pounds (80 kilograms) of food every day. That's twice its body weight.

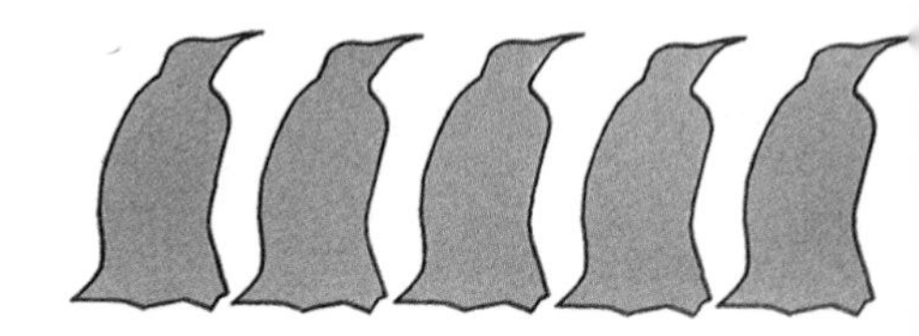

African elephant—5.9 tons (5,400 kilograms)

An African elephant eats about 768 pounds (349 kilograms) of food every day. That's more than 6 percent of its body weight.

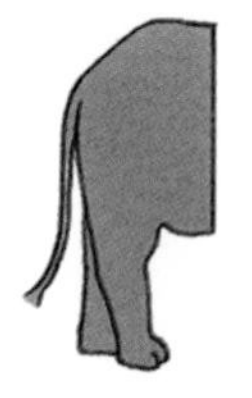

2.7 tons (2,443 kilograms) in a week

Etruscan shrew—0.07 ounce (2 grams)

An Etruscan shrew eats about 0.2 ounce (6 grams) of food every day. That's three times its body weight.

Find out more by looking at pages **38–39**
42–43

How do living things get energy?

Living things get energy from their food. Food contains various substances that include **sugars.** Sugars are chemicals that contain stored energy. As the substances in food are digested and broken down into tiny pieces, the sugars join with oxygen that is inhaled from the air. This process releases the energy in the sugars and makes it available for the body to use.

The sugars contain a substance called **carbon**, which is an element found in all living things. Energy is released when the oxygen that is inhaled joins chemically with the carbon in food. The joining of carbon and oxygen also produces the gas carbon dioxide, a waste product. The carbon dioxide is then exhaled.

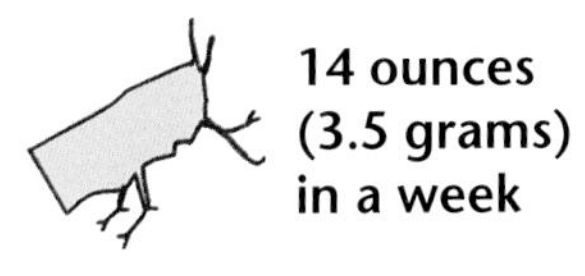

14 ounces (3.5 grams) in a week

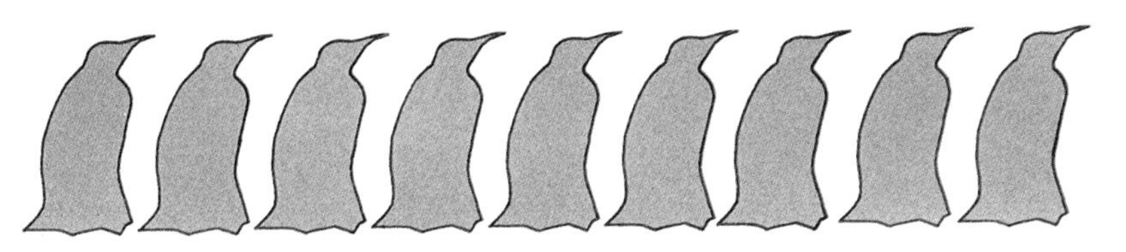

1.23 tons (560 kilograms) in a week

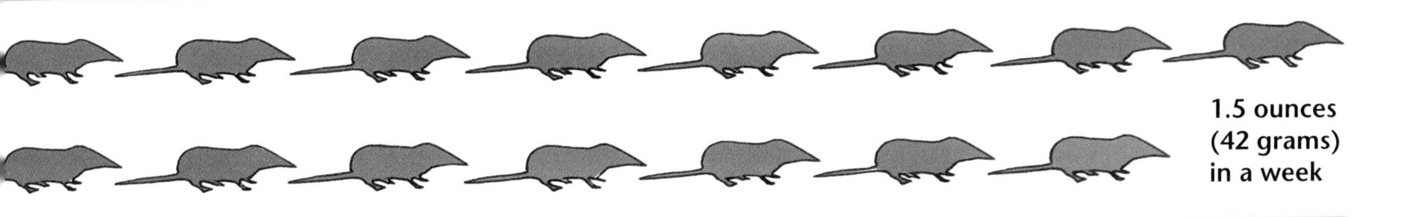

1.5 ounces (42 grams) in a week

Essential supplies

Did you know that digested parts of the food you eat are carried to your fingers and toes? In fact, they are carried all around your body. The different parts of your body are made up of many tiny cells. Cells need a supply of food to keep them alive and well. They also need a supply of the oxygen you inhale from the air.

This is true of most animals and plants. The cells inside them need a supply of food and oxygen. But how is the food and oxygen carried to all the different parts of the animals and plants?

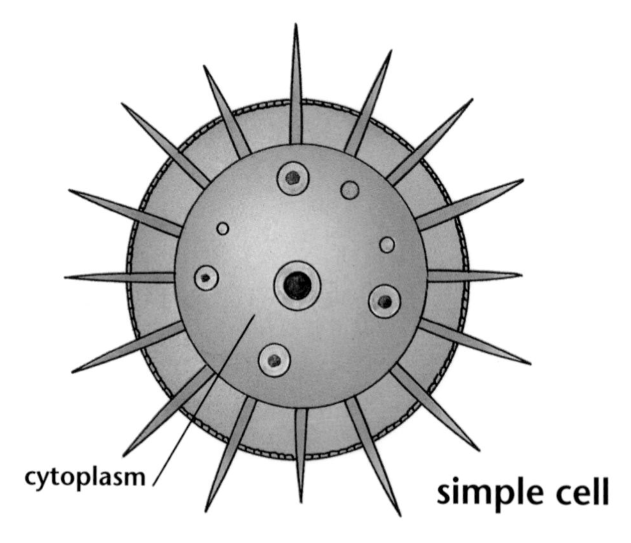

In a single-celled organism, food is carried around by the moving cytoplasm.

Blood makes the delivery

In most animals, food and oxygen are carried around the body by the **blood.** The blood is pumped around and around the body by the heart. As the blood travels, it picks up oxygen from the lungs. It picks up digested food from the stomach, intestine, and a special store in the liver. It then carries the oxygen and digested food products to all the cells as it moves around the body.

Cells are tiny living things and, like other living things, they produce waste. The waste substances are carried away from the cells by the blood as it moves through the body.

In mammals, blood travels around the body inside tubes called **blood vessels.** Birds, reptiles, and fish also have blood vessels. But the blood of insects flows around their body openly instead of in blood vessels. The blood fills up the insides of their body and supplies the cells with food. But it does not take oxygen to the cells like blood does in other animals. Insects take in oxygen through tiny holes in the sides of their body.

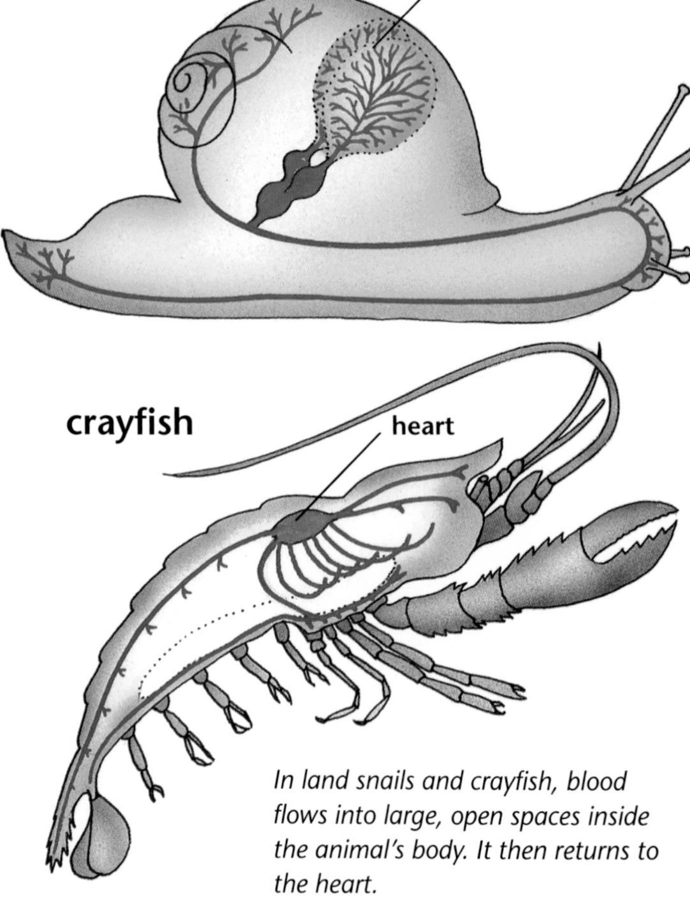

In land snails and crayfish, blood flows into large, open spaces inside the animal's body. It then returns to the heart.

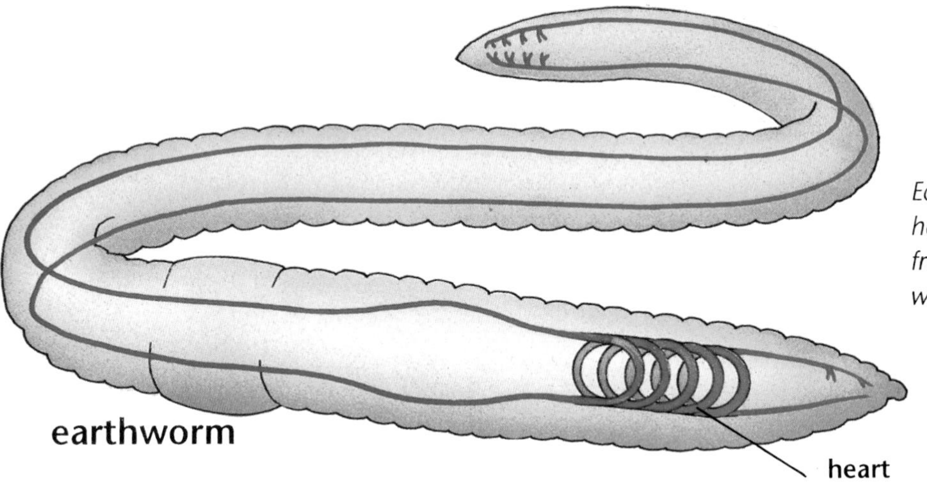

Earthworms have five pairs of hearts! Blood vessels branch out from the hearts to supply the body with blood.

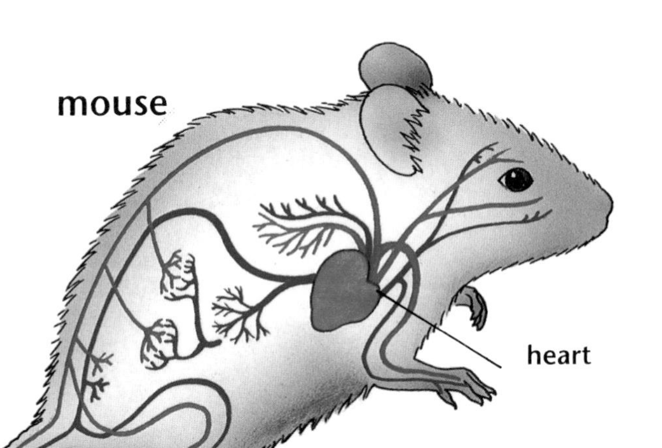

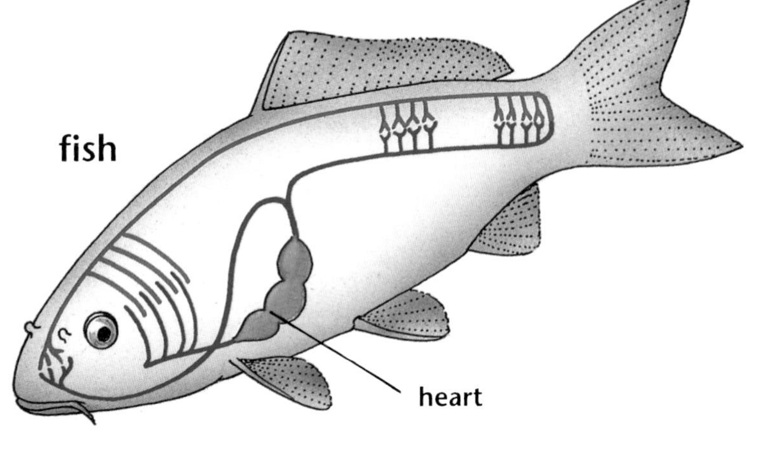

In mice, blood is pumped from the heart and travels through the body inside the blood vessels. In fish, blood is pumped from the heart to the gills before traveling to other parts of the body.

What is plant sap?

In plants, food has to travel from the leaves, where it is made, to other parts, such as the stems and roots. Plants have a juice inside them called **sap.** The sap is like the blood of the plant. In many plants, it flows through special tubes called **phloem,** which carry the sugars in the sap to all the plant's cells.

In other plants, another kind of sap containing water and minerals is carried by special vessels called **xylem** from the roots of the plant up to its leaves.

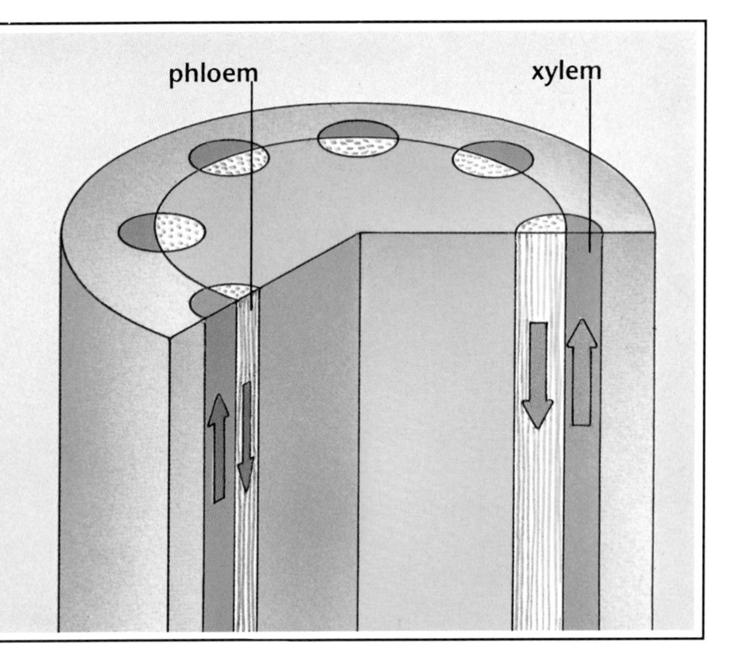

Moving about

When an insect flies, its wings beat up and down. These wing movements are controlled by different muscles in the insect's body. In turn, these muscles become tight or relaxed.

Some of the muscles in your body are joined to bones. They make the bones move at places where they meet each other, called **joints.** The muscles do this by becoming shorter and fatter. This makes them pull at the bones so that they move. Muscles can only pull—they can't push. This means that muscles of this kind have to work in pairs. One pulls the bone one way and the other pulls the bone back again. In your arm, your **biceps** makes your elbow bend, and a muscle called the **triceps** pulls your arm straight.

You need your muscles to make your body move. Other animals also need their muscles, so that they can catch their food, protect themselves, and do many other things. Muscles can make bodies run, walk, turn, bend, fly, and swim.

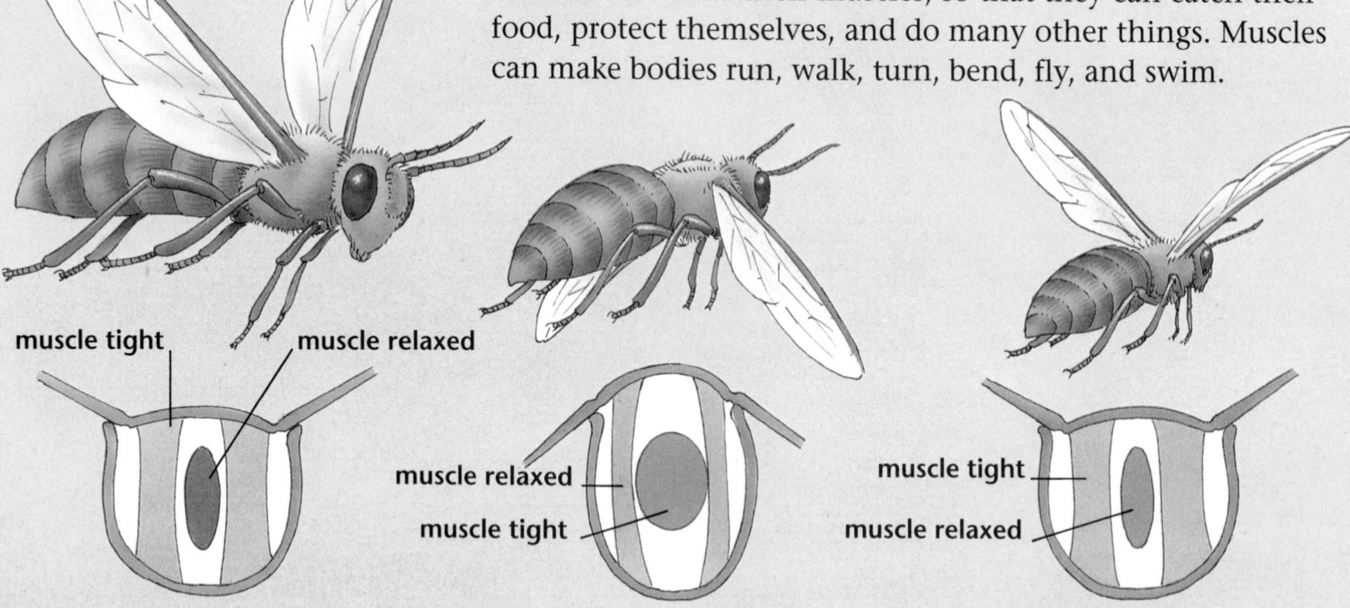

Feel your muscles!

1. Hold up your left arm, as shown in the picture.

2. Place your right hand on the upper part of your left arm.

3. Now clench your left fist against your left ear. You will feel the muscle moving. This muscle is the biceps.

Bones help, too!

Human beings and many other animals have their bones inside their body. But some animals have their bones on the outside. You may have seen a beetle crawling up a blade of grass. Inside the beetle's legs, there are tiny muscles just like yours, which pull the animal's legs backward and forward. You can't see its muscles moving because they are inside a hard outer casing called the **exoskeleton.** The beetle's muscles are firmly attached to the inside of its exoskeleton.

Not all animals have both hard bones and muscles to make them move. Earthworms do not have bones. They use their muscles to crawl. The earthworm stretches the front part of its body and then pulls up the back part to move along.

Watching animals move

If you watch small animals walk across a sheet of plastic, you can see more clearly how they move.

1. Ask an adult to help you find some small animals and a sheet of plastic. Ask the adult to hold the plastic safely for you.

Be careful that the animals you have chosen are not poisonous.

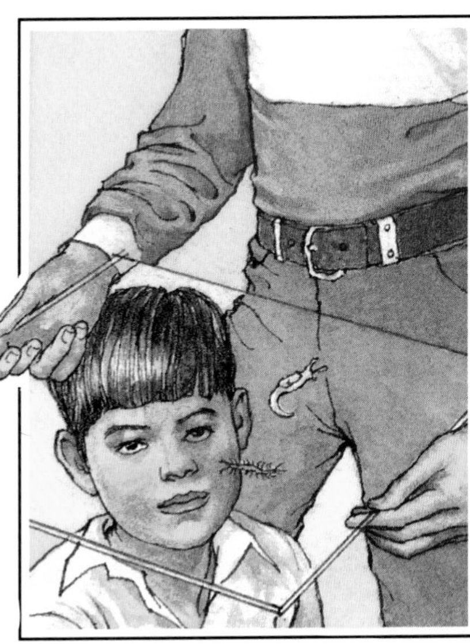

2. Place the animals on the plastic, and then look at them from below. This way, you can see the movements very clearly. Write your observations in your notebook.

You will need:

a sheet of clear plastic, such as acrylic

some small animals, such as wood lice, earthworms, snails, and beetles

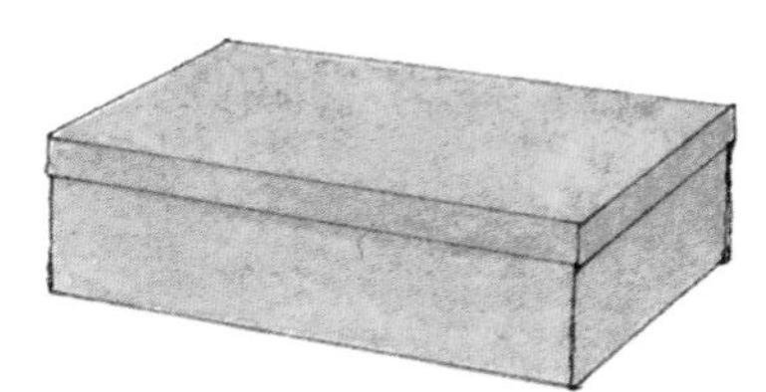

a cardboard box

Keep the animals in a dark, cool box while not in use. When you have finished with the animals, take them back to the place where you found them.

Keeping in touch

When you turn the pages of this book, you are moving your hands and fingers. As you read, your eyes are moving as they follow the words on the page. These body movements are happening because you are making them happen. You could easily stop them if you wanted to. This kind of body movement is called a **voluntary movement.** Voluntary movements of the body are all the movements that you make your body do, such as walking, running, or picking up a pencil.

Your body also moves in another way. While you are reading this book, your heart is moving as it beats. Parts of your stomach and intestines are moving as they digest your food. You do not make these body movements happen. They are automatic. This kind of body movement is called an **involuntary movement.**

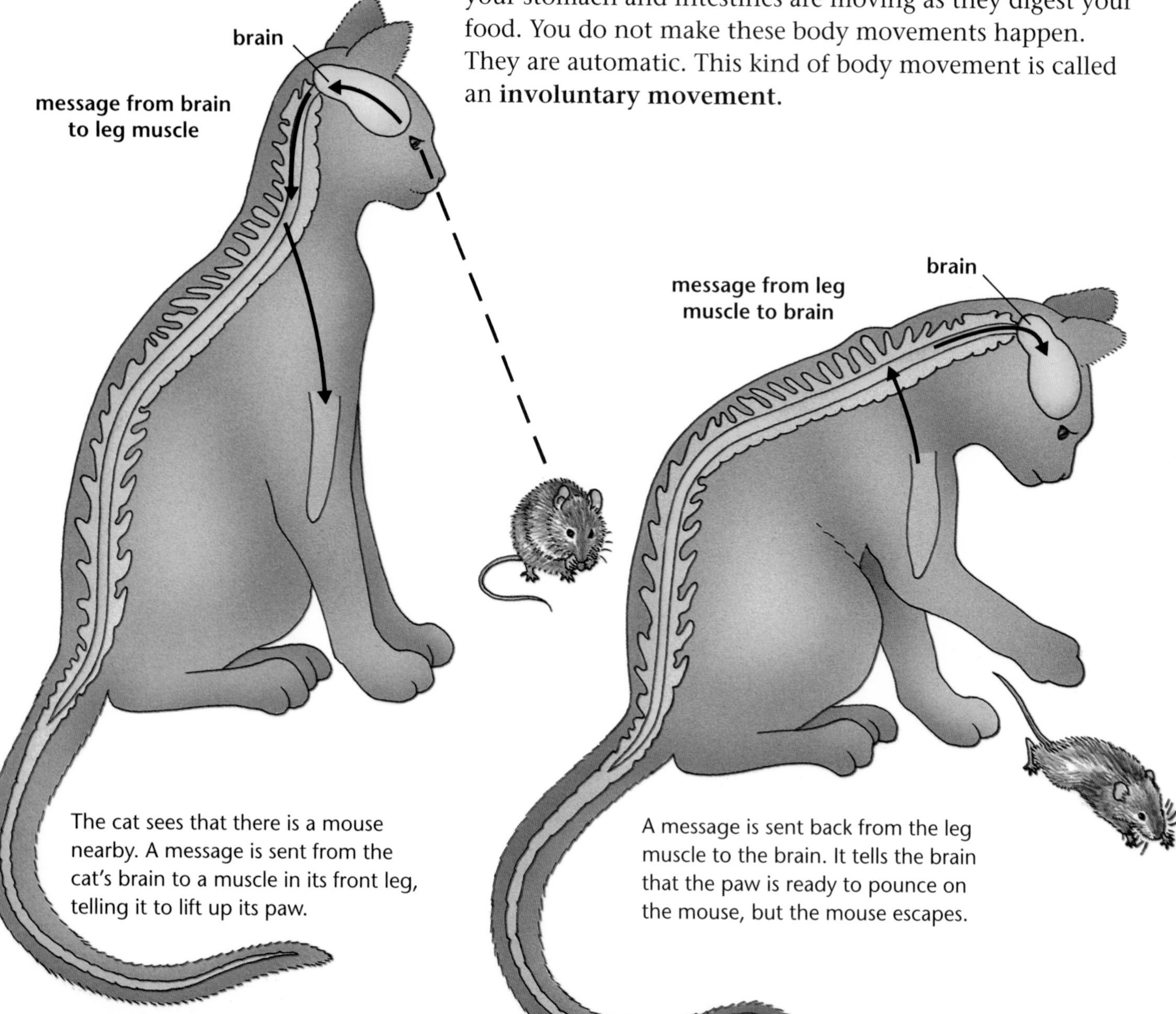

The cat sees that there is a mouse nearby. A message is sent from the cat's brain to a muscle in its front leg, telling it to lift up its paw.

A message is sent back from the leg muscle to the brain. It tells the brain that the paw is ready to pounce on the mouse, but the mouse escapes.

What does the nervous system do?

How do the parts of your body know when to move? Your brain sends them messages through a network of nerve cells that make up the **nervous system.** When you decide to pick up a pencil, your brain sends a message through the nervous system to the muscles in your arm and hand to start moving. The nervous system also carries messages to the parts of your body that move without your control, such as your heart and stomach.

Most animals have some kind of nervous system. But no animal has a brain as well developed as the one in human beings. When animals are in danger, messages travel through the nerve cells to tell the different parts of their body what to do. If a mouse sees a cat, messages will be sent quickly through the nerve cells of the mouse to tell it to run away. In the same way, a snail will pull its head into its shell for protection when it senses a threat.

Chemical messages

There is another way that messages are passed around the bodies of human beings and other animals. This way involves the use of chemical substances called **hormones.** Most hormones are made in organs of the body called **glands.** These glands are found in various parts of the bodies of human beings and most animals. An important gland is the **pituitary gland.** This is often called the master gland. It lies just beneath the brain and produces many different hormones.

Hormones help to control digestion, growth, and other body functions. For example, when you are eating, digestive hormones in your stomach help control the flow of digestive juices into the stomach. These juices help break down the food into simple substances that can be used by the body.

The pituitary gland lies just beneath the brain. Although it is only the size of a pea, it produces many different hormones and is one of the most important glands.

Find out more by looking at pages **20–21**

What is reproduction?

Human beings have babies. Fish lay eggs, which hatch into young fish. Trees produce seeds, which can grow into new trees. Living things make copies of themselves. This is the process of **reproduction.**

Asexual reproduction

There are two different kinds of reproduction. In one kind, there is only one adult of the species, and the young ones look exactly the same as their parent. This kind of reproduction is called **asexual reproduction.** Living things reproduce like this in several different ways.

The simplest living creatures reproduce by just **splitting** in two. Most creatures that are made up of only one cell reproduce in this way. Even some simple animals such as sea anemones, whose bodies are made up of many cells, can do this.

Many plants can make new plants from a small piece that has broken off, such as a twig or stem. This is useful if the plant has been damaged by animals or by strong winds. It is also useful to gardeners, because it means that they can take **cuttings,** which grow into new plants. The plants grown from cuttings will be exactly the same as the parent plant.

The underground stem of the cowslip sometimes develops new stems. After a few years, the oldest part of the stem dies, and the plants are separated.

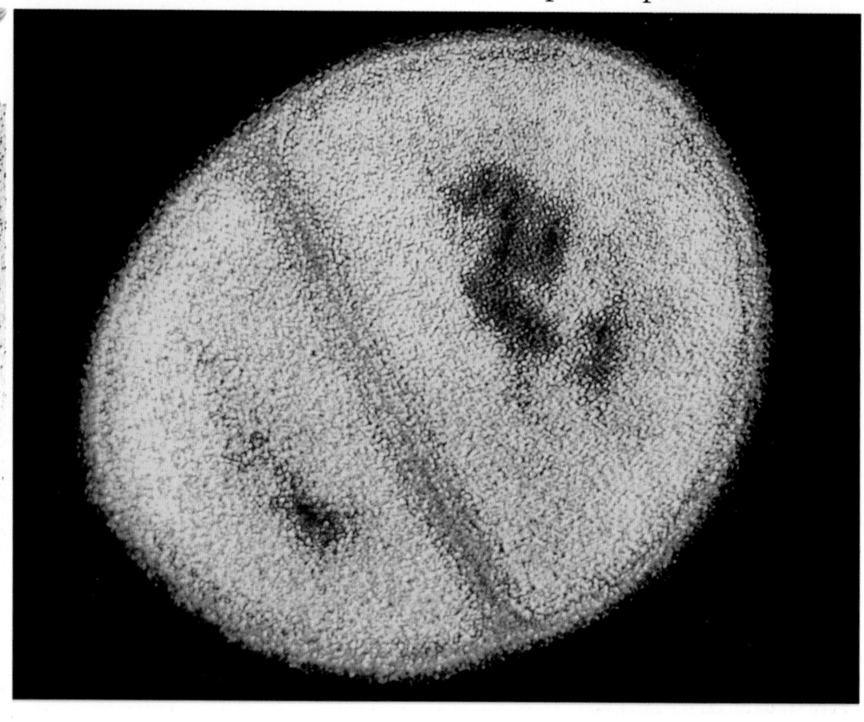

This bacterium is in the process of dividing into two. It does this by itself, without the help of another bacterium.

The male bullhead fish guards eggs from predators.

Sexual reproduction

In **sexual reproduction**, there are two adults of the species—one male and one female. The young ones are not quite the same as the parents. Human beings reproduce in this way. You don't look exactly like your parents, though you may look a bit like both of them. This is true of other animals and plants with two parents. They get some of their features from one parent and some from the other.

For sexual reproduction to take place, one cell from the male must unite with one cell from the female. In animals, the male produces cells called **sperm** and the female produces **egg** cells. When one egg cell joins with one sperm cell, **fertilization** is accomplished. The fertilized egg then begins to develop into a new organism.

Fertilization can happen inside or outside the female's body. In most fish and frogs, the female lays eggs and the male releases his sperm over them. In birds and mammals, the male's sperm **fertilizes** the eggs inside the female's body.

In plants, the male cells are called **pollen.** Pollen is carried from male flower parts to female flower parts, usually by insects or by wind. The pollen fertilizes the egg cells and produces seeds, which grow into new plants. In many plants, the male and female flower parts are in the same plant.

Find out more by looking at pages **18–19**
26–27

What is a parasite?

Animals feed on other animals or plants or both. But some small animals actually live on, or even in, the animals or plants from which they feed. They eat small amounts of the living bodies of larger animals or plants, which also provide shelter for them. Animals that do this are called **parasites.** Some plants are parasites, too. They grow on other plants and feed from them. They don't make food for themselves as other plants do. The animal or plant that parasites live on is called the **host.**

Animal parasites

Some animal parasites feed by sucking the blood of larger animals. These blood-suckers include ticks, fleas, lice, and leeches. One of these parasites clings to the body of the host animal and bites into its skin. The parasite's body becomes swollen as it fills with blood. Fleas jump from one part of the host animal to another, sucking its blood.

Fleas live in clothes and on the bodies of humans, birds, and other animals. They suck the blood of a host animal.

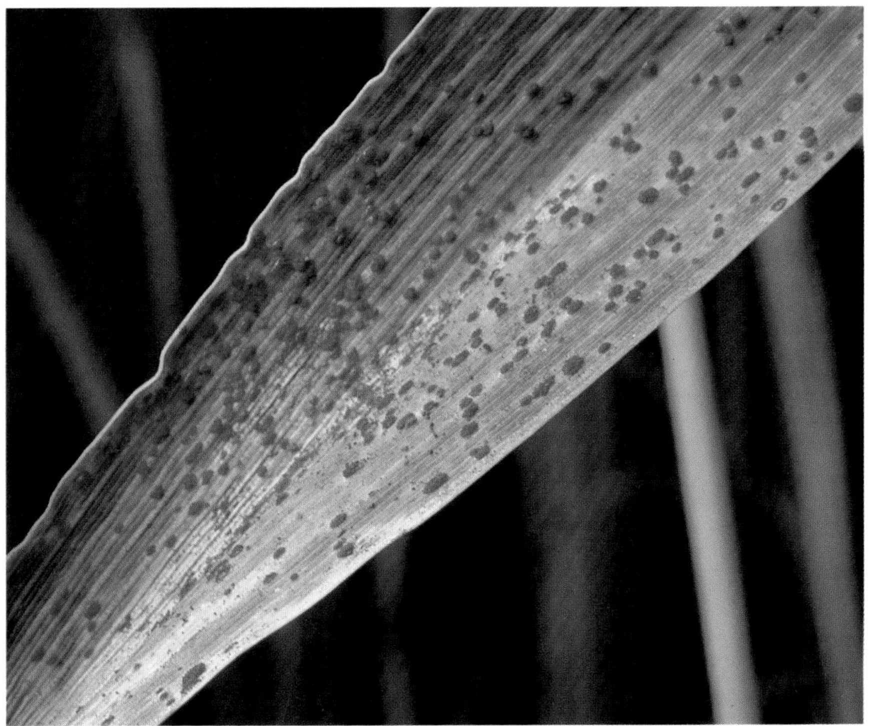

Plant parasites can do great damage to crops. This stem rust is a fungus growing on a barley leaf.

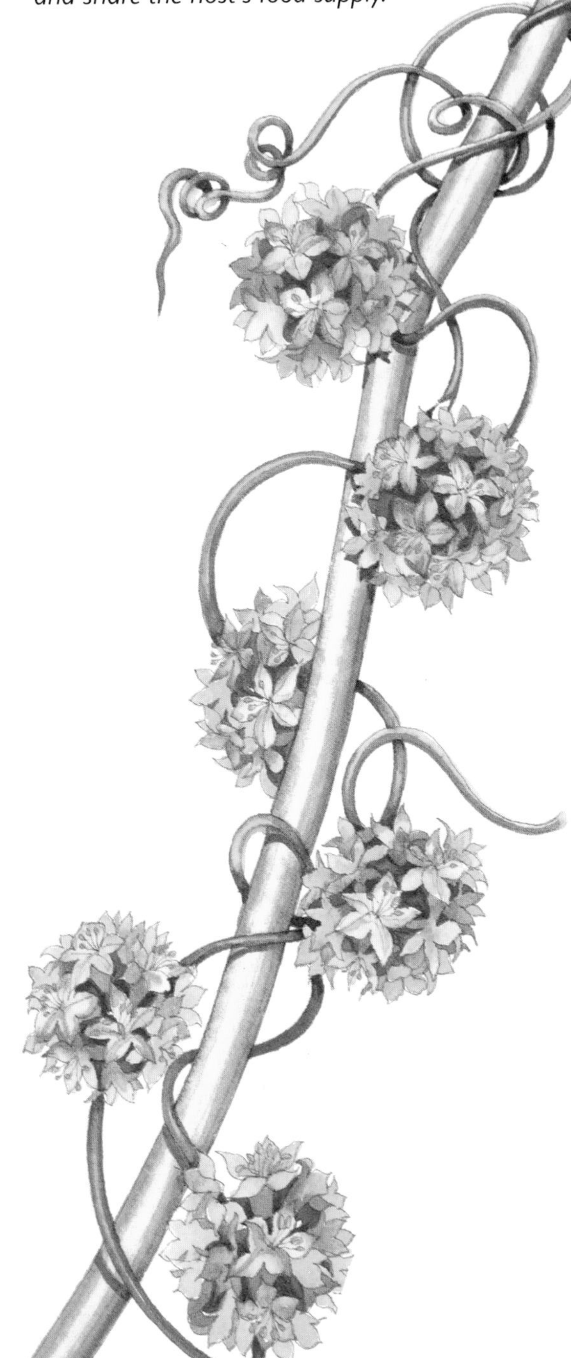

Dodder stems wrap themselves around a host plant. Special suckers become attached to the host plant and share the host's food supply.

Plant parasites

Many plants that are parasites, such as dodder or rafflesia, don't have green leaves. And they don't have green stems as other plants do. Other plants are green because they contain a green substance called chlorophyll. This absorbs the sunlight they need to make their food. Plants that grow and feed on other plants don't make their own food.

Fungi

Some kinds of fungi are parasites. Fungi can grow on plants and animals and can cause serious diseases. The fungi that grow on plants can sometimes spread very quickly and destroy important crops, such as wheat and potatoes.

The smallest parasites

Parasites that feed on people and animals cause many diseases. One type of ameba causes a painful disease called amebic dysentery in people. Other protozoans cause diseases such as malaria. Blood-sucking insects pick up these tiny parasites from infected animals and pass them on to other animals and people. Most bacteria are parasites, also. Bacteria cause diseases such as tuberculosis and pneumonia.

Defenses

Most animals and plants live in danger of being killed or harmed by other living things. So they have to have some way of defending themselves. A species of plant or animal with no protection would not survive.

Inner protection

Animals and plants can defend themselves against harmful bacteria and viruses. Animals have special cells that fight and kill these bacteria and viruses. These cells are ready to protect any part of the body that is attacked.

When an animal's skin is pierced and bacteria enter the wound, **white blood cells** quickly crowd into the hurt area. The cells destroy the harmful bacteria by surrounding and attacking them. The broken skin is gradually repaired by new skin cells that grow across the wound.

Plant cells have strong walls to keep out bacteria and viruses. But when insects feed on plants they break down the cell walls. Bacteria and viruses can then enter the plant and cause disease.

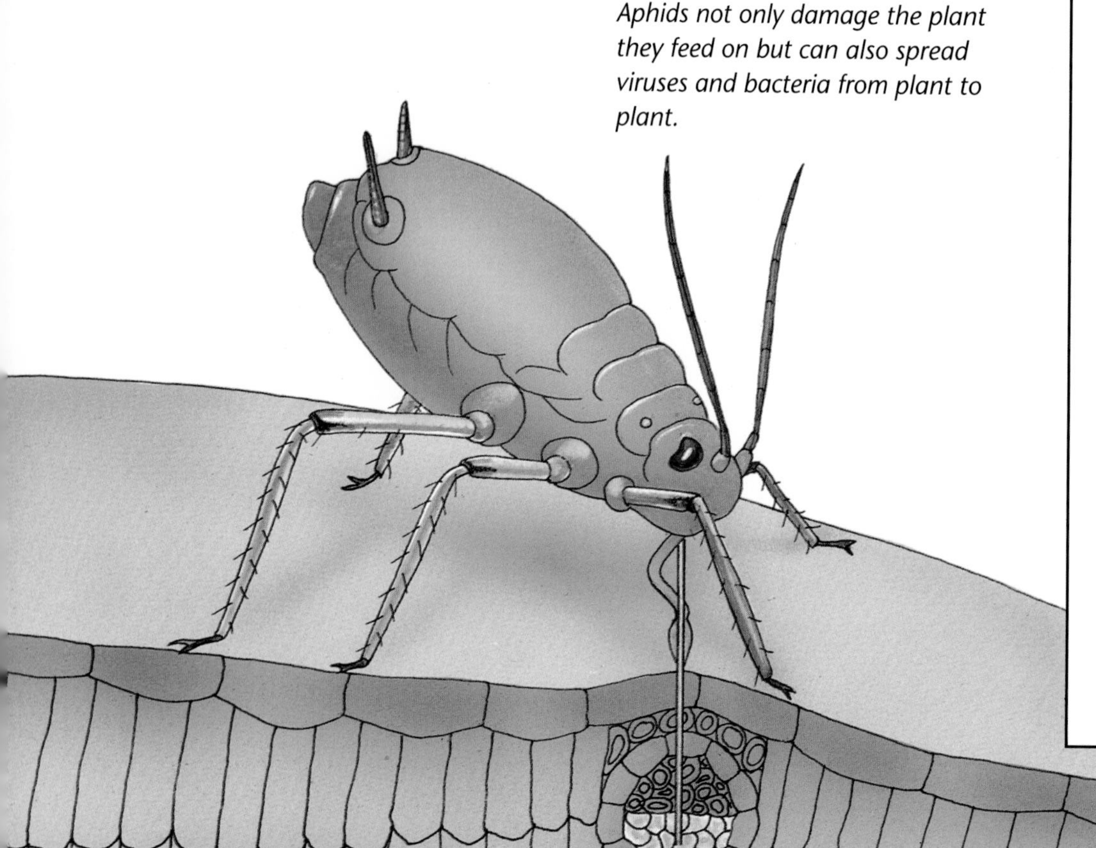

Aphids not only damage the plant they feed on but can also spread viruses and bacteria from plant to plant.

Fighting infection

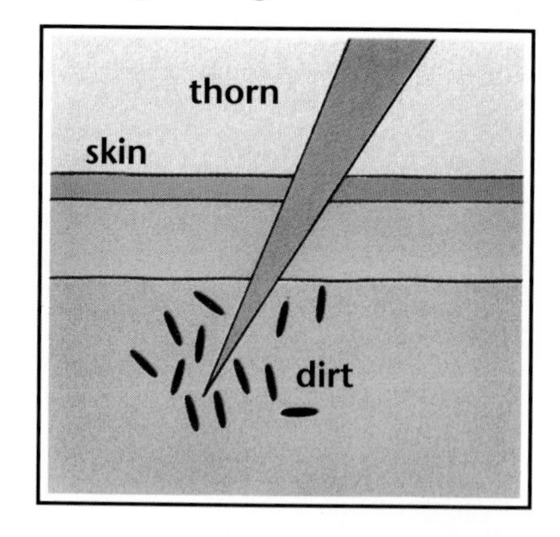

1. A thorn digs into the skin of an animal, letting in dirt and bacteria.

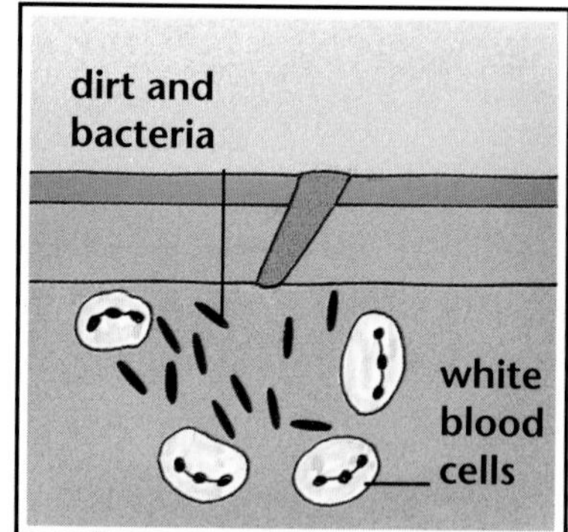

2. White blood cells cluster around the wound.

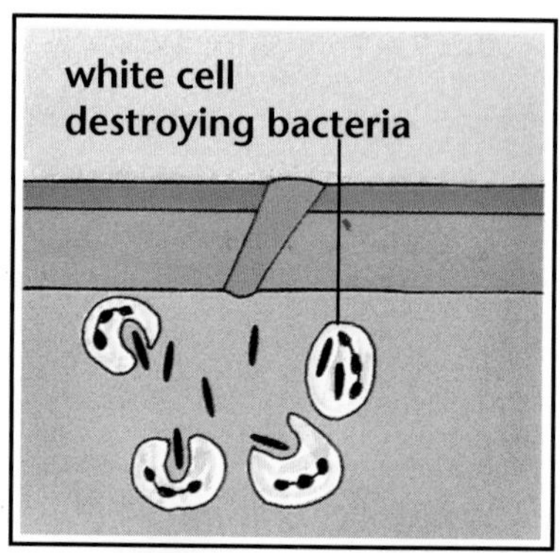

3. Some white cells destroy the bacteria by "eating" them.

Find out more by looking at pages **18–19**
36–37

The spines of cactus plants provide good protection from animals who might want to eat the plants.

Outer protection

Insects need good ways of defending themselves because there are so many larger animals that can eat them. Bees and wasps can inject poison into their enemies with their sting. Many ants have a poisonous bite or sting. Plants cannot move so they need special protection, such as prickles, thorns, hairs, or tough skins.

Warning colors

Poisonous insects are often brightly colored. Red and black or yellow and black are the most common colors found on these creatures. To other animals these colors mean, "Stay away!" They are called **warning colors.**

Camouflage

Many animals defend themselves by blending in with their surroundings. This is called **camouflage** (also called cryptic coloration). When they keep still, some insects look like twigs, leaves, or flowers.

This fossil of a reptile was found in Switzerland. The animal probably lived about 200 million years ago.

Then and now

Rocks often contain the remains of living things that died long ago. These remains are called **fossils.** The kinds of rock that contain most fossils are called **sedimentary rocks.** Sedimentary rocks build up in layers very slowly. So we know that the rocks near the surface, just under the soil, are younger than the layers of rock below them. The oldest rocks are right at the bottom. By studying elements in the rocks, scientists can tell how old they are.

1. This prehistoric fish probably lived in the ocean about 400 million years ago.

2. When the fish died, its body sank down to the ocean floor.

3. Sand and mud covered up the fish's body. The flesh decayed, and the remainder of the body became a fossil.

Secrets in the rocks

Rocks that formed less than 300 million years ago contain fossils of all kinds of different animals and plants, including horses, tigers, birds, dinosaurs, dragonflies, and flowers. In rocks that are between 500 million and 300 million years old, fewer animals and plants have been found, though there are plenty of fossils of fish, plants without flowers, and simple animals such as mollusks.

Older rocks, made over 500 million years ago, contain no vertebrate fossils. The oldest animal invertebrate fossils are about 700 million years old. These animals include very simple creatures like jellyfish and worms. The oldest fossils are about 3.5 billion years old. These fossils are of very primitive bacteria.

Scientists believe that **fossil records** show that life began with very small, simple creatures. As time went by, more and more complex creatures appeared. The most complex animals and plants—mammals, birds, and flowering plants—appeared last of all.

This trilobite looks similar to a modern wood louse. Trilobites lived in the sea.

Find out more by looking at pages **58–59**

Survival

Some scientists believe that living things developed from other simpler living things, which have slowly become more complex over millions of years. There are enough fossils to show clearly how some kinds of animals have changed over time. Studying fossils has helped scientists to reach the conclusion that mammals have branched off and followed reptiles. Other fossils show what the ancestors of some animals, such as the camel, looked like. Camels developed from a line of small animals the size of a fox. Camels then developed as larger animals with hooves, a long neck, and large teeth.

The animals that became better suited to their surroundings are the ones that have survived. The giraffe's long neck, for example, enables it to reach high up into trees and eat the leaves there. Scientists believe that animals have survived because their ancestors were the ones that could make best use of their surroundings.

Some animals, such as the dinosaurs, were not able to survive. No one knows exactly why they died out. Other species have also disappeared completely. Some were hunted until they became extinct. Others have been wiped out by disease, or changes in climate, or the destruction of their native habitat.

Over millions of years, bigger and heavier elephants appeared. The mammoth was about 15 feet (4.5 meters) tall. There are now only two kinds of elephant—the African and the Indian elephant. The African elephant is about 11.5 feet (3.5 meters) tall.

How living things have developed

Different forms of living things have developed over millions and millions of years. Scientists believe that the first living things appeared about 3.5 billion years ago.

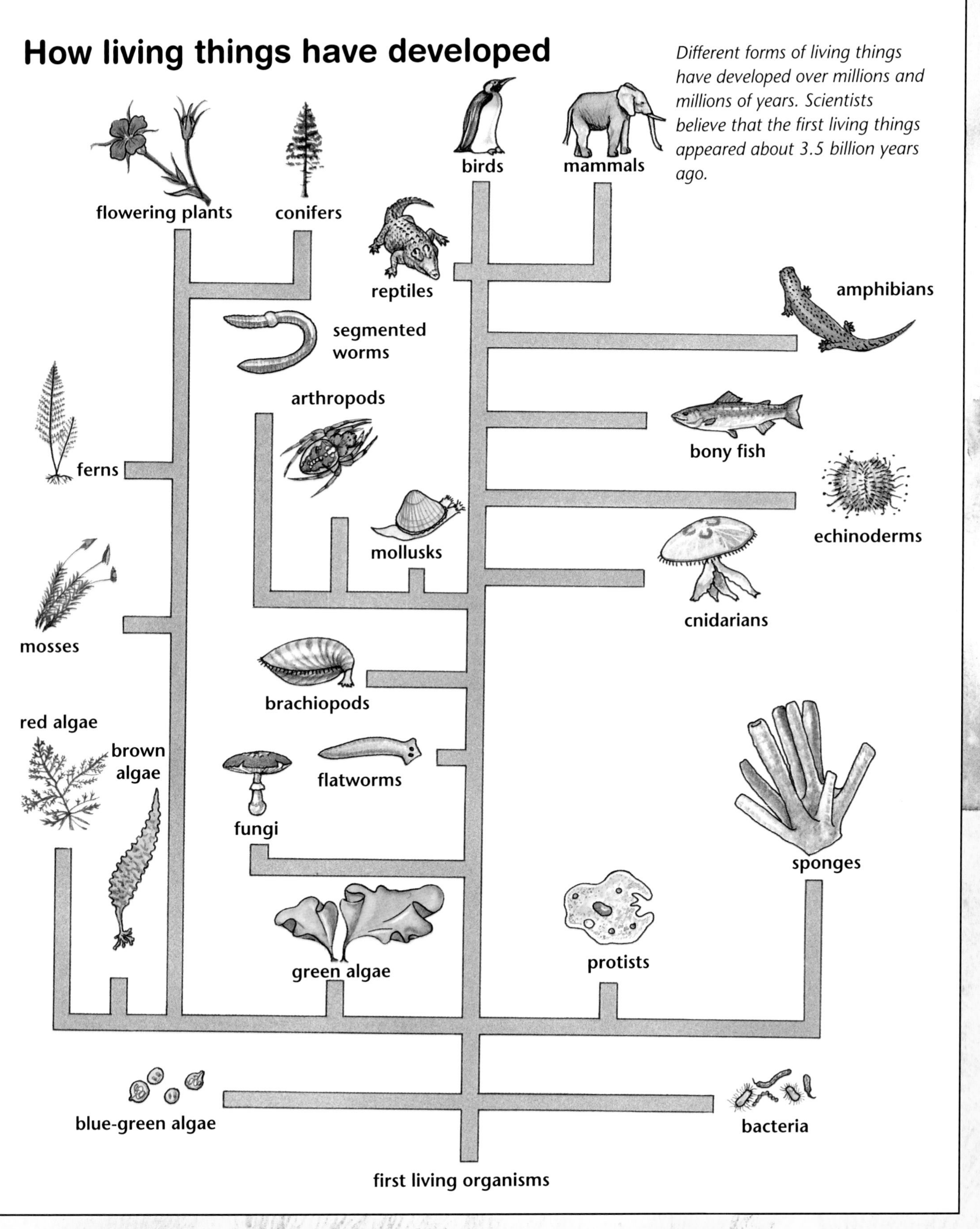

PLANTS

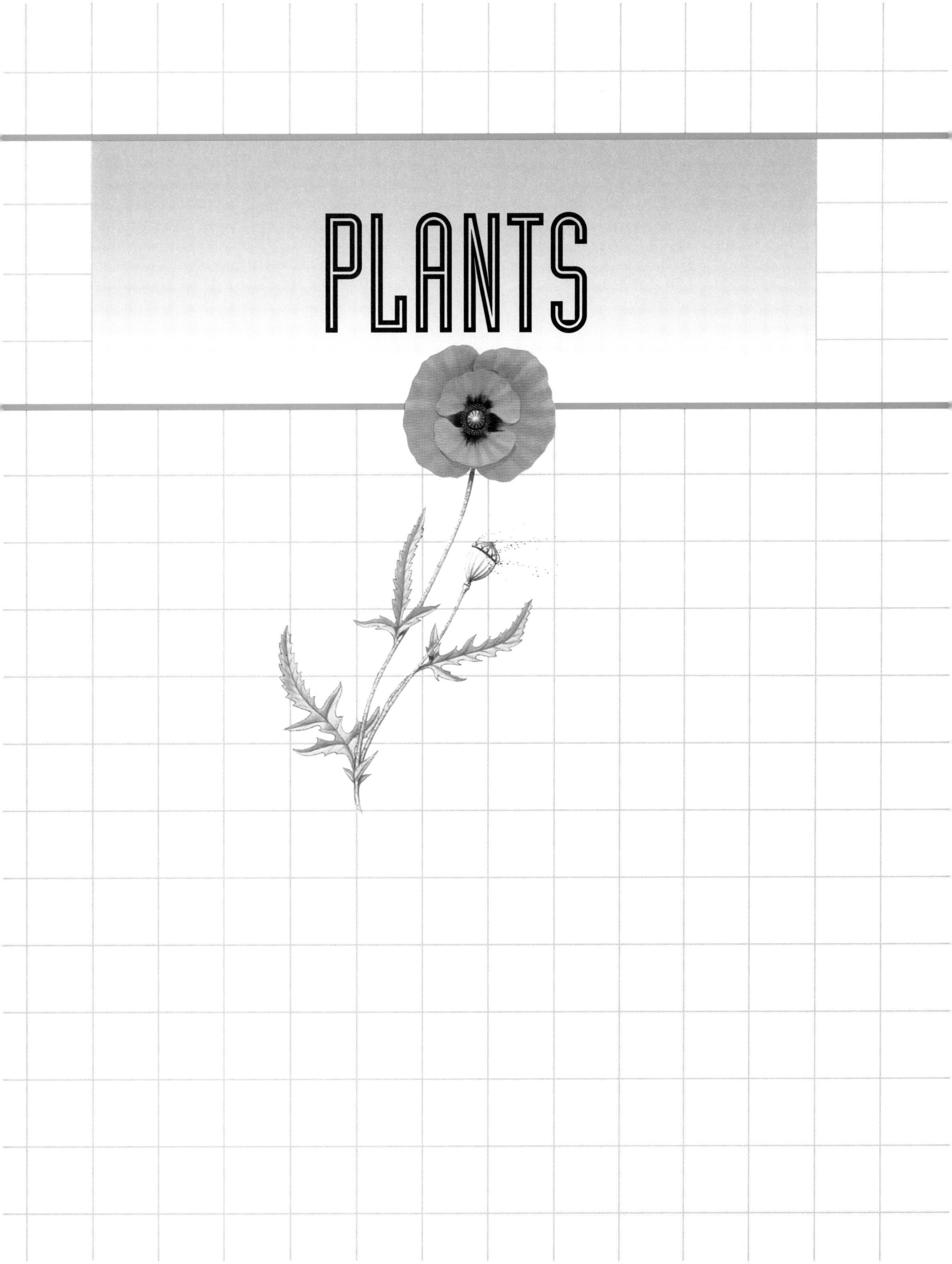

These are all plants!

Do you like climbing trees? Or looking at flowers? Or eating fruit? If so, you like plants! Scientists who study plants are called botanists. Botanists have discovered and named 260,000 different kinds of plants—and they find new ones every year. Botanists classify their discoveries, that is, sort them into groups based on the features they have in common. This system helps the botanists keep track of their discoveries.

Most of the world's plants can be placed into five groups. These groups are: 1) seed-bearing plants, 2) ferns, 3) lycophytes, 4) horsetails, and 5) bryophytes. Can you find each of these groups on these pages?

Ferns have leaves called fronds

Horsetails have hollow, jointed stems

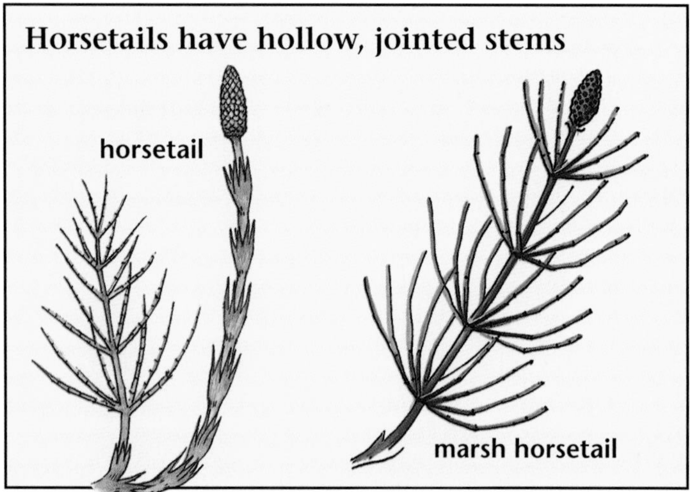

Lycophytes have leaves with a single, central vein

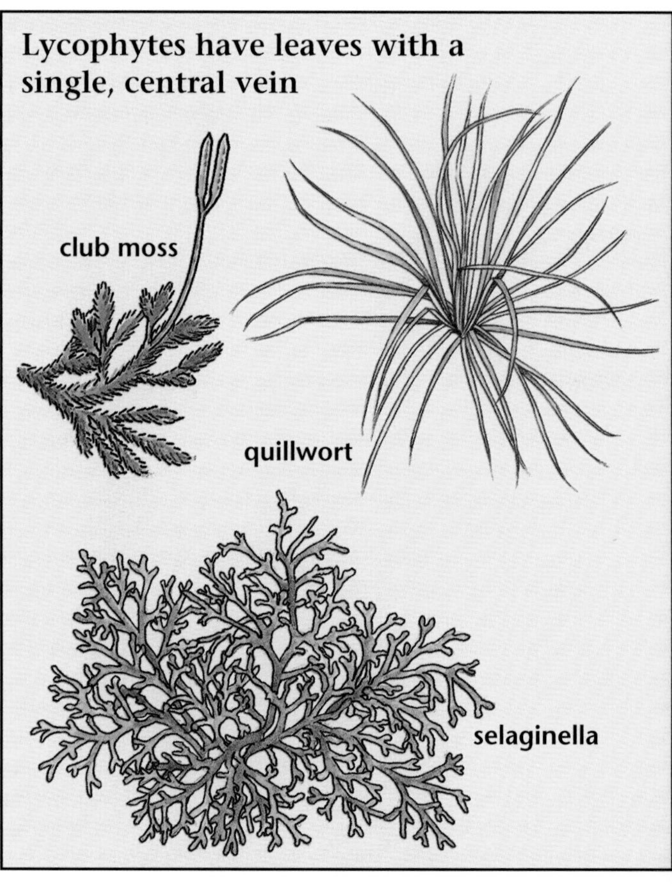

Bryophytes lack true roots

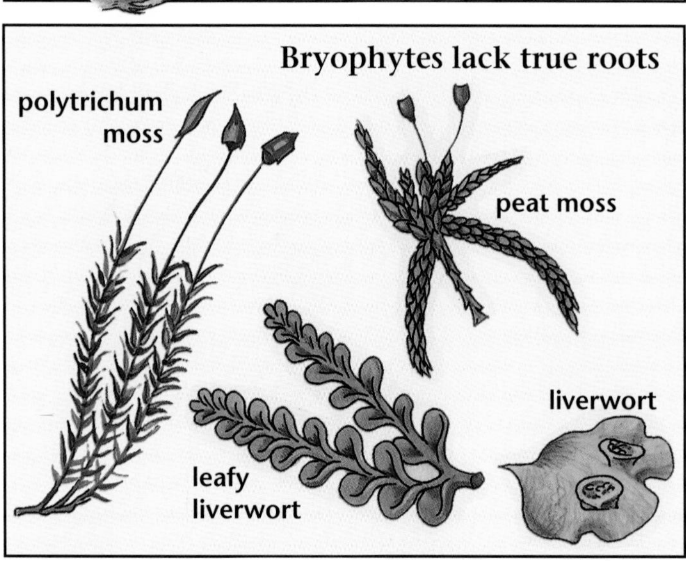

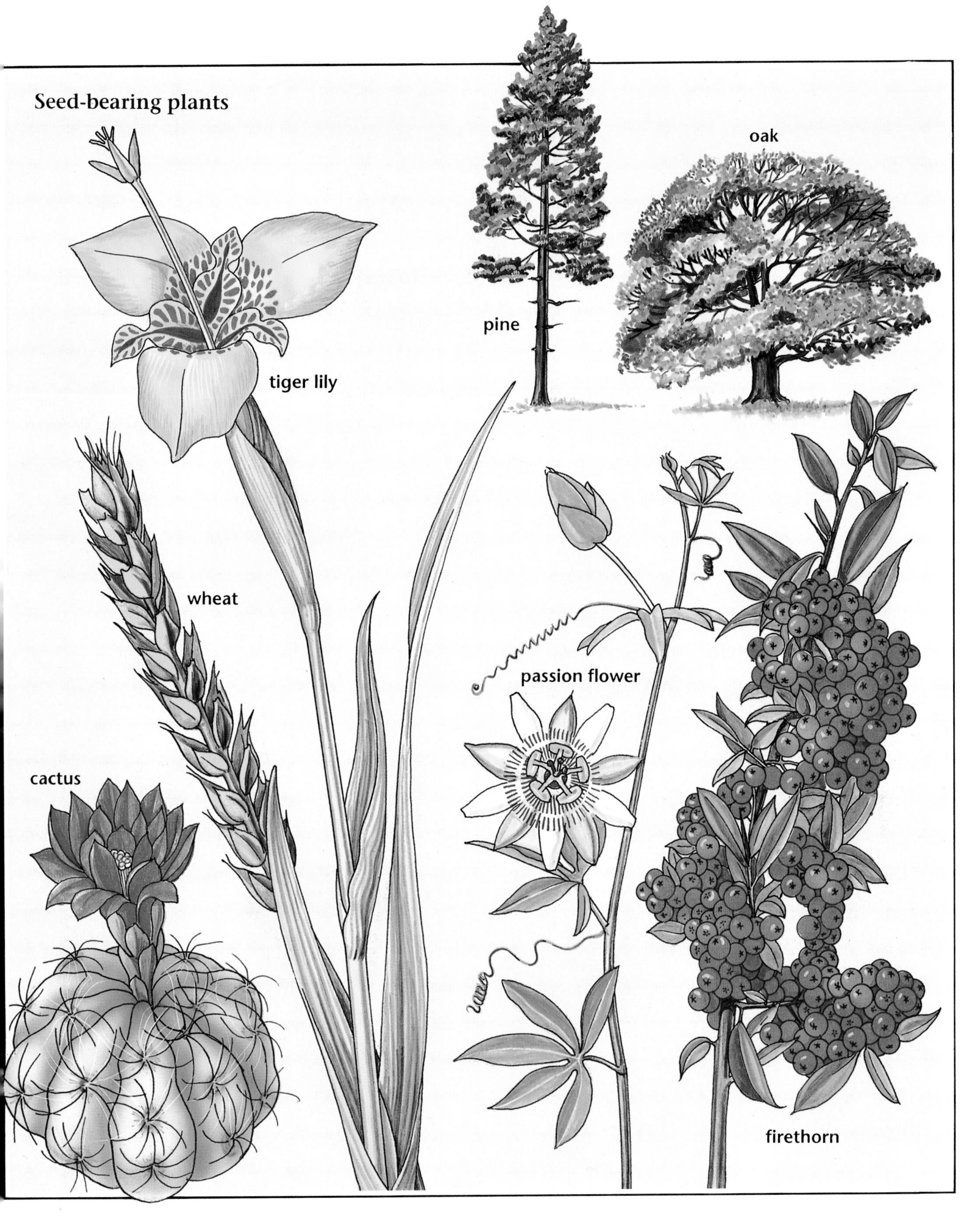
Seed-bearing plants
oak
pine
tiger lily
wheat
passion flower
cactus
firethorn

Find out more by looking at pages **84–85**
104–105
112–113

Plants in wet places

Did you know that plants can live almost anywhere? Most plants like warm temperatures, lots of rainfall, and soil that has plenty of nutrients. But there are many other plants that survive in areas where it's very cold, or very hot, or very wet. How do they do it?

Over thousands and thousands of years, many small changes have taken place in plants that allow them to live in certain places. This process is called **natural selection.** That's why you can find plants living in water, near the North Pole, and in the hottest desert!

Water plants

Some flowering plants, such as water lilies, and certain grasses, such as rice, can live with most of their parts under water. They have developed networks of spaces in their leaves, stems, and roots. Oxygen can enter the spaces through **stomata** (holes) in the leaves. The gas is also produced inside the chloroplasts during photosynthesis. Oxygen can spread though the spaces right down to the roots!

Water plants collapse as soon as they are taken out of water because they need it to hold up their stems and leaves. The stems are flexible and bend with the flow of the water so that the plants are not damaged by strong currents.

The leaves of giant Amazonian water lilies float on the surface of the water. They can support the weight of birds, such as this jacana bird.

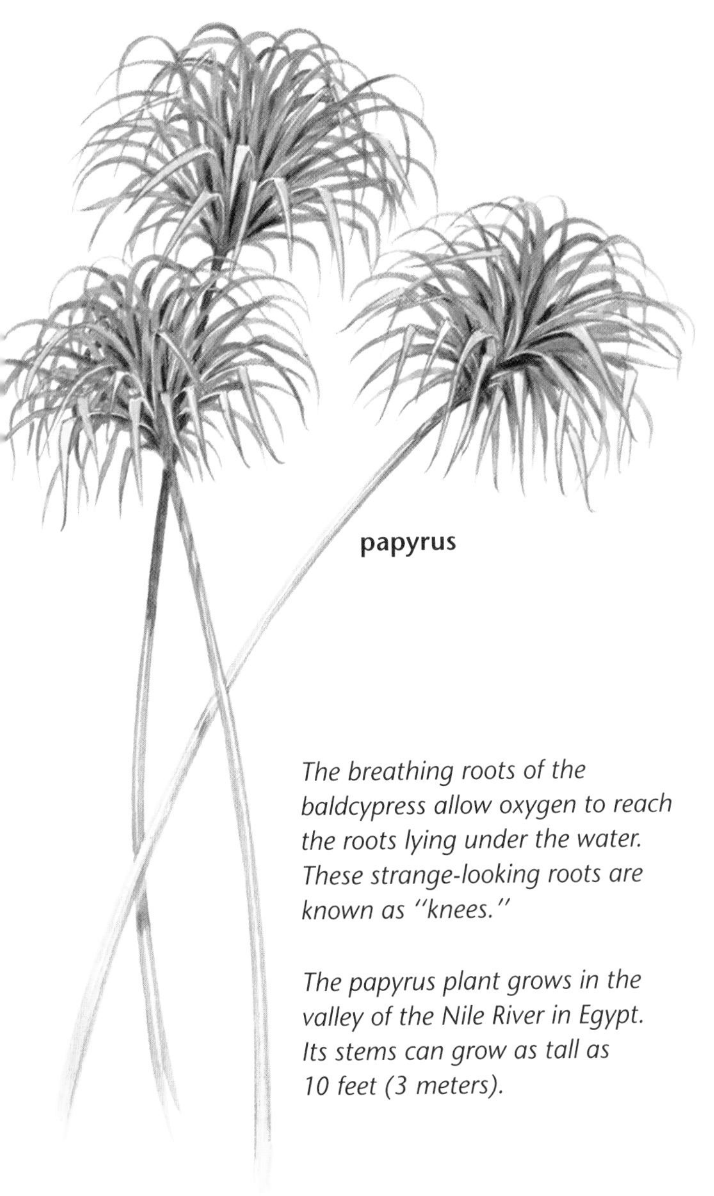

The breathing roots of the baldcypress allow oxygen to reach the roots lying under the water. These strange-looking roots are known as "knees."

The papyrus plant grows in the valley of the Nile River in Egypt. Its stems can grow as tall as 10 feet (3 meters).

Round-leaved crowfoot is found growing in water pools in moors, which are large areas of open wasteland. The leaves are divided into three segments and float on the surface of the water.

Swamp plants

Freshwater **swamps** are special kinds of inland places where water collects because it can't drain away. When there is a great deal of rainfall, the ground becomes waterlogged. Some swamps always have a layer of water covering the ground. Most swamp plants have their roots in water, but their stems and leaves grow above it.

Some trees that grow in swamps have special breathing roots to take in the oxygen they need. The baldcypress is a large conifer that grows in the southern United States. It has breathing roots that grow upward from the soil like miniature tree trunks. These breathing roots are hollow in the middle to allow air to flow down below the water to the normal roots deep in the mud.

Saltwater marshes and swamps

Although many plants live in or near the fresh waters of rivers, lakes, and streams, salt water is quite another matter! Many plants cannot survive in places where the water contains a lot of salt. Plants that live near the sea have had to develop ways of coping with, or tolerating, a lot of salt. Botanists call these plants **halophytes.** Many halophytes live in saltwater marshes and in swamps that are covered by seawater when the tide comes in.

Which plants like salty water?

Plants such as marsh samphire and seablite live in saltwater marshes. These halophytes are able to tolerate salty water because they have salt glands that get rid of the excess salt from their shoots.

Sea lavender and some other halophytes that live in saltwater marshes are perennials, which die down each year. They get rid of any excess salt in their old stems and leaves. Sea lavender is so good at tolerating salt that its seeds don't germinate unless they're in seawater!

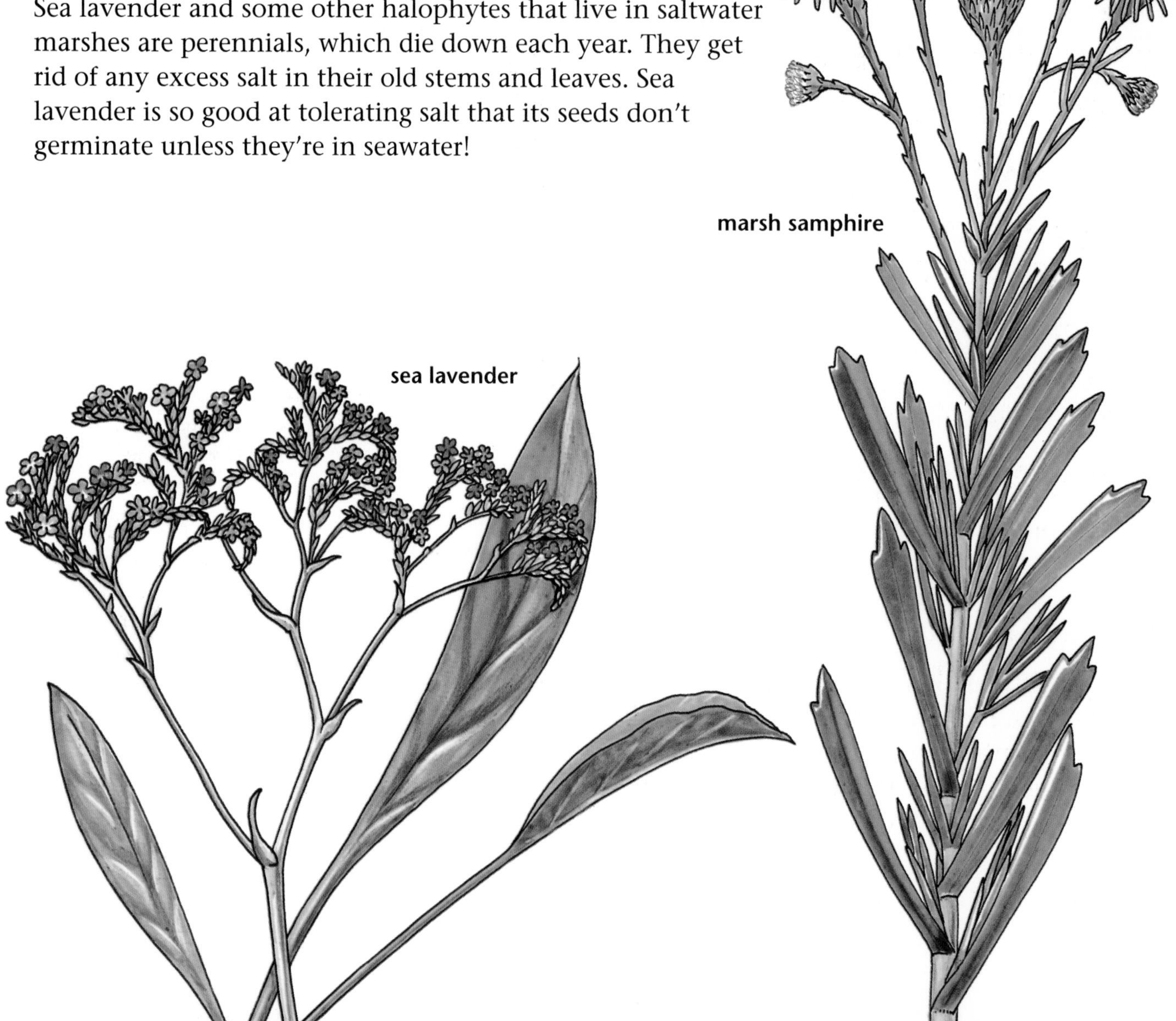

The arching roots of this Brazilian mangrove tree are firmly fixed in the mud below.

Mangrove swamps

Tidal swamps in tropical areas are often called **mangrove swamps** because most of the trees that grow there are mangrove trees. Mangrove trees have arched roots that hold them firmly in the mud as the tide goes in and out.

The seeds of some kinds of mangrove trees germinate on the parent tree. A root grows from the seed, becoming as long as 1 foot (30 centimeters). When the seed falls from the tree, this root helps the seed to float upright in the water. If the root tip strikes mud, a new mangrove tree may begin to grow.

Plants that don't like salt

You will need:

two pieces of blotting paper or paper towels

some mustard seeds

water and salt

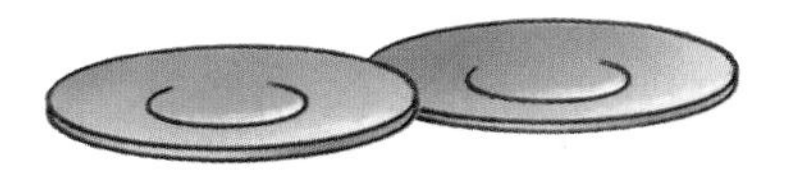

two saucers

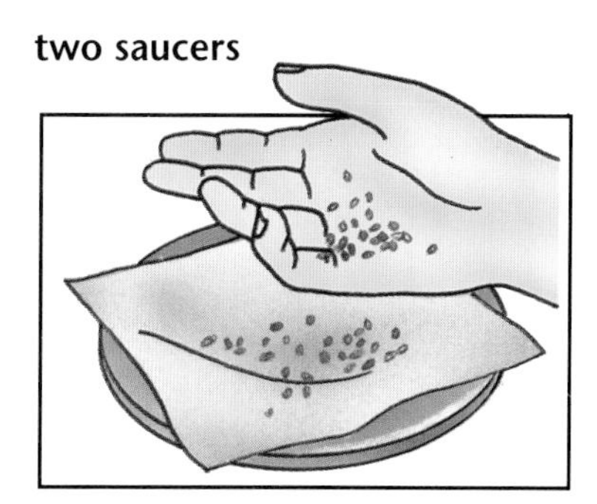

1. Cover each saucer with a piece of blotting paper or paper towel. Moisten the paper with fresh water. Sprinkle some mustard seeds on each saucer.

2. When the shoots are about 1 inch (2.5 centimeters) tall, water them again. This time use fresh water for one saucer, but mix salt in the water for the other saucer. Label the saucers "fresh" and "salt."

These plants don't like salt, so the ones that are given saltwater will die. The plants that have fresh water will keep on growing.

Find out more by looking at pages **100–101**

Plants in dry places

Grasses, low shrubs, and wild flowers grow in the Arctic tundra of Alaska. Most tundra plants grow slowly and some do not flower until they are at least 10 years old.

Can you name two kinds of **habitat**, or places to live, where the shortage of water limits the kinds of plants able to grow there?

Tundra plants

A **tundra** is a cold, dry region where trees cannot grow. But mosses, grasses, and wild flowers grow there. So do lichen and various kinds of animals. There are two kinds of tundra, Alpine and Arctic.

Alpine tundras are on mountains at altitudes where trees cannot grow. The soils of most tundras are well drained. Various kinds of animals, like deer and sheep, graze there in the summers.

In Arctic tundras, there's plenty of water, but the area is so cold that for most of the year the water is frozen solid as snow and ice. For two or three months every year, the tundra warms up enough for the ice to melt. But the ground is still frozen solid, so the tundra is dotted with thousands of pools.

A dwarf willow in the Arctic tundra grows very slowly. A stem no thicker than a pencil may be 100 years old!

The growing season for tundra plants is so short that they can grow only a small amount each year. These plants grow in small clumps, which protects them from the wind and cold.

These flowers are growing in the hot, dry conditions of the desert.

Desert plants

Another dry habitat is the **desert**, where it rains only occasionally. The water that falls in the desert quickly dries up again in the hot sun, so desert plants have to be able to survive on very little water.

Cactuses and other **succulent** plants grow roots that spread out a long way, but only just below the surface of the ground. When it rains, the roots quickly take up a lot of water in a short time, as much as possible before the ground dries up again. Some cactuses swell up with a store of water that will provide all the moisture they need for many months.

Do you know how the spines on a cactus help to keep the water in? Some animals try to eat cactuses to get at the water, but are stopped by the sharp spines. Some cactuses are covered in shaggy hair that helps stop water from being lost.

Even though the soil near the surface may be dry, there is often water deeper underground. The mesquite tree that grows in American deserts has roots that descend as deep as 66 feet (20 meters) to reach the water there.

Plants in woods and forests

What kinds of trees are growing in the woods or forests near your home? Some trees have leaves that stay green all year long. These are **evergreen** trees. Other trees have leaves that change color and fall every year. These are **deciduous** trees.

Many evergreens keep their leaves for several years, growing new ones before shedding the old ones.

What is an evergreen?

In most parts of the world, some trees are able to keep their leaves all year. They can tolerate dry conditions because of their small, waxy leaves. The leaves of some evergreen trees are leathery and tough so that they aren't damaged by harsh, cold winds. Others are thin and sharp, like tiny green needles. These leaves are not damaged by freezing cold air. Some of these leaves fall each year but are replaced by new leaves. That is why pines, spruce, holly, eucalyptus, and most acacias are called evergreens.

Making bark rubbings

Most trees and shrubs have an outer covering called **bark**. You can see the pattern of a tree's bark by making a bark rubbing.

You will need:

large sheets of white paper

a large wax crayon

1. Hold a piece of paper firmly against the bark of a tree.

2. Rub the wax crayon over the paper, and the pattern of the bark will appear. Can you find out what kind of tree it is by the pattern of its bark? Use a tree identification book.

3. Keep a record of your rubbings in your notebook.

Falling leaves

Deciduous trees that live in seasonally dry or cold places protect themselves by becoming **dormant** (inactive) and by losing all their leaves. These trees can be compared with hibernating animals.

As the cold or dry season starts, all the food in the leaves moves into the stem and roots of the tree. A corky layer grows at the base of the leafstalk and the leaves turn brown, yellow, red, or other colors before falling off. When the weather becomes warm and moist again, new green leaves will grow.

Throughout the temperate regions of Europe, North America, and Asia, deciduous trees, such as oak, ash, maple, birch, and beech, lose their leaves before the cold season begins.

In North Africa and around the Mediterranean, and even in the drier parts of the tropics, many trees lose their leaves every year to help the tree survive the dry season.

The largest and tallest living things

Conifers (cone-bearing plants) include the largest and tallest living things in the world. Among the largest living things are the giant sequoia trees of California. The largest giant sequoia measures about 275 feet (83.3 meters) high and has a circumference of about 103 feet (31.4 meters) at the base of its trunk. That's so thick that you could hide a bus behind it! The tallest trees are the redwoods that grow in the United States. The tallest known living tree in the world, a redwood tree in Redwood National Park in California, reaches about 368 feet (112 meters) high.

Deciduous trees, such as this Norway maple, lose their leaves during the cold season. The leaves change color to yellow and orange before falling off.

Plants in the rain forest

There are millions and millions of trees in huge forests that grow in hot, wet places, such as the Amazon in South America, the Congo in central Africa, and parts of India, Malaysia, and New Guinea. The temperature in these places is usually about 77 °F (25 °C) all year round, and as much as 33 feet (10 meters) of rain may fall there in a year. These forests are called **tropical rain forests.**

What grows in the rain forests?

The moist, warm conditions in a rain forest provide an ideal habitat for plants to grow. A greater variety of plants grows in the rain forests than anywhere else on Earth.

Most of the trees in the rain forest are evergreens. Many grow as tall as 153 feet (46 meters) high, and their leafy branches link up to form a green layer as much as 33 feet (10 meters) thick. This layer at the top of the trees is called the **canopy.** A great many smaller plants and most of the animals live in the canopy, because few can survive on the ground. The canopy shuts out most of the light, and the forest floor is a dark, damp habitat.

Large areas of tropical rain forests are being destroyed by people who want to clear the land for farms and cities. Scientists fear that this destruction will cause many species of plants and animals to become extinct.

In the tropical rain forests, the trees grow so close together that very little sunlight reaches the ground. Many plants, such as orchids, grow high up in the trees.

Climbing plants

Among the plants that live in the rain forest are climbers called **lianas.** These are rooted in the ground but grow up the tree trunks and around the canopy. Thousands of other plants, called **epiphytes**, grow by attaching their roots to the branches of trees, not to the ground. Epiphytes don't harm the trees because they don't take any food from them. Instead, they soak up water through their own leaves and stems, and they get all the mineral nutrients they need from animal droppings and decaying leaves.

This pink bromeliad plant is a kind of epiphyte. It is growing on a tree trunk in the Brazilian rain forest.

Plants of the chaparral

Chaparrals are found in the Mediterranean region, from southern California into parts of Mexico, and in parts of Chile, southern Australia, and South Africa.

A **chaparral** is an area where the winters are mild and wet, and the summers are hot and dry. Chaparrals are found in the Mediterranean region, from southern California into parts of Mexico, and in parts of Chile, southern Australia, and South Africa. If you hiked across a chaparral, you would see mostly shrubs and small trees. Sometimes, the trees and shrubs grow so close together on the chaparral that you couldn't even walk between them.

Fire!

Fires often break out during the long, hot summers on the chaparral. Many shrubs in these areas contain thick juices in their leaves called **essential oils**, which makes them catch fire easily.

These fires are actually a good thing. They help clear areas that are too thickly grown. The burning exposes the ground to the sun and makes way for new plant growth.

Manzanitas are a common shrub on the chaparral, above. They have bell-shaped flowers in the spring and red fruit in the fall, right.

Find out more by looking at pages **108–109**

Trees, shrubs, and vines

Chaparrals are one of the few areas where shrubs are the main form of plant life. Can you tell the difference between a shrub and a tree?

Shrubs are smaller than trees, even when they are full grown. Shrubs also have many stems that grow close to the ground. A tree has one main stem, called the **trunk.**

A shrub is different from a vine because it can stand up on its own and doesn't climb. Vines grow by climbing along a support.

Botanists say that trees and shrubs, and some vines, are "woody." A plant is "woody" if its stems and branches don't die off in winters where the climate is cold.

A vine is a climbing plant that needs support to grow.

A tree is a large plant with a single stem called a trunk.

A shrub is a smaller plant with many stems that grow close to the ground.

Plants of the grasslands

Nearly every continent in the world has huge areas where grasses are the most common plants. Different types of grasslands have different names. **Steppes**, like those in the Ukraine, have short grasses. **Prairies**, which include much of the American Midwest and the pampa of Argentina, have tall grasses. Tropical **savannas**, like those in the Sudan, have coarse grasses.

These grasslands are often destroyed by fire. They quickly grow again when conditions are suitable. Many smaller plants also spring up at this time, from bulbs and seeds which were dormant in the soil. Many plants of the daisy and pea families grow here. Some have seeds that cannot germinate until they are scorched by fire.

Most grasslands are in areas of low rainfall. Grasses are well suited to dry conditions. Their roots can take in moisture when the soil is wet and save it for the dry season.

What's beyond the grasslands?

There is rarely a sharp boundary between grassland and the vegetation of surrounding areas. Near an area of more rainfall, bushes and then trees are found scattered in the grassland. They become more and more numerous as the habitat changes to woodland or forest. Near an area that receives less rainfall, the grassland becomes more sparse until it becomes stone or sandy desert.

This is a typical African savanna scene during the dry season in Kenya. Acacia trees grow in the Australian and African savannas, and in parts of North and South America.

How does grass grow?

As you grow bigger, you grow all over. Your whole body grows, though your head grows less quickly. Similarly, plant leaves grow from young, small ones into old, big ones. But stems have growing points only at the tips of shoots and where a leaf joins the stem. If you cut the tip off a stem, the plant will grow new twigs lower down on the stem.

Grasses and many of their relatives have growing regions just above each joint of the stem. If the top of the grass is cut off, for example, when it is eaten by an animal, it will grow again by branching at a lower joint.

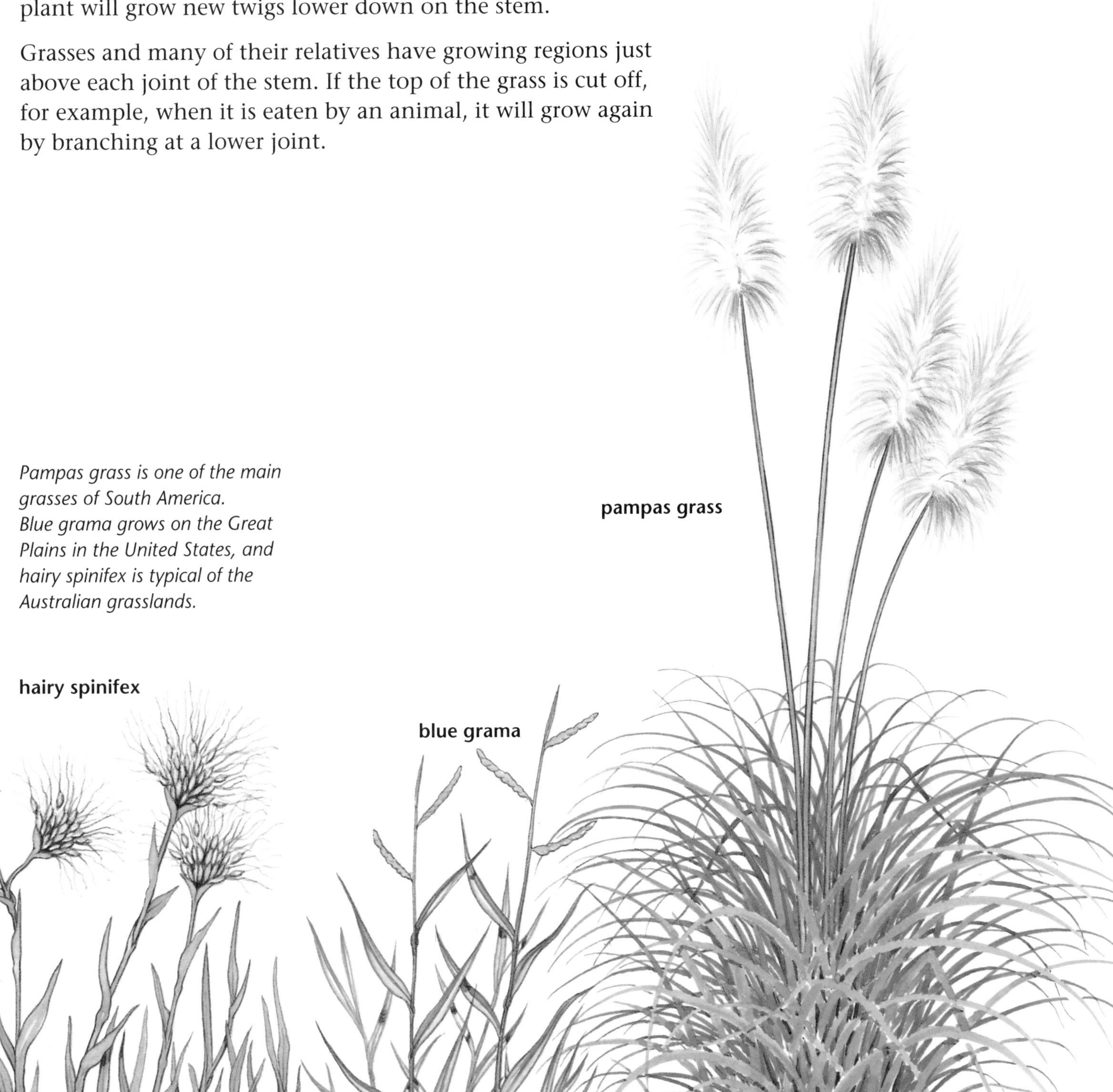

Pampas grass is one of the main grasses of South America. Blue grama grows on the Great Plains in the United States, and hairy spinifex is typical of the Australian grasslands.

Extraordinary plants

Fog often rolls in from the sea and floats across the Namib Desert in southern Africa. The water droplets in the fog provide moisture for the welwitschia plant. The water is absorbed by the younger parts of the welwitschia's leaves. The stem of the welwitschia is cone-shaped and partly buried in the sand. Two leaves grow from the rim of the stem. The first section of these long leaves is broad and flat. The older parts split into lots of thin ribbons. Welwitschia plants grow very, very slowly—only a few inches every hundred years!

A killer plant

The strangler fig kills other plants and makes room for itself to grow! The strangler fig is a tree that grows in Southeast Asia. Birds eat the fruits of the fig and then drop the seeds on the branches of another tree. When a seed germinates, its long roots grow in twisted shapes around the other tree and down to the ground. As the roots of the strangler fig grow bigger and stronger, they crush the bark of the other tree and cut off its supply of food. Then the strangler fig keeps on growing while its victim dies.

A sensitive plant

The mimosa plant is so sensitive that its leaves suddenly fold up and droop if something touches them. Sometimes it takes as long as half an hour for the mimosa leaves to stand firm and upright again.

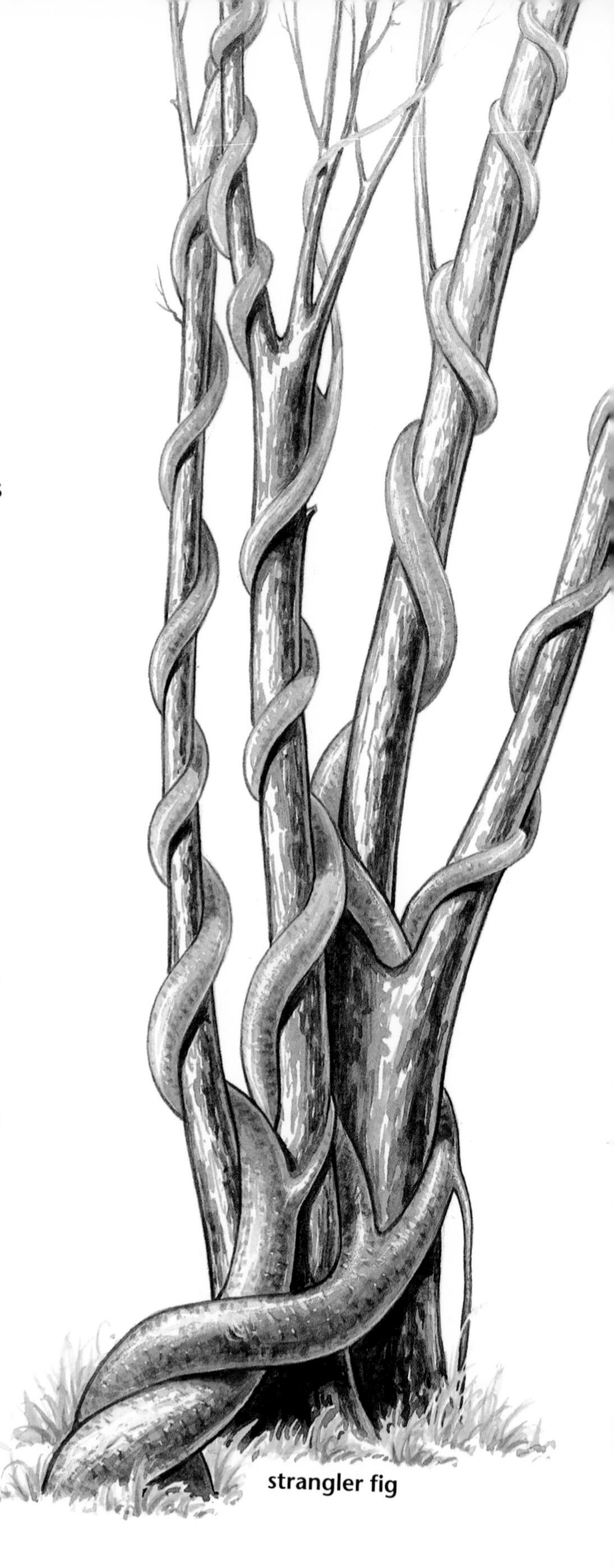

strangler fig

Some plants eat insects

Most plants can get the minerals they need from the soil or water that they grow in. But other plants live in places such as bogs. A bog is a kind of wetland where the soil is high in acid, but low in oxygen and minerals. The insects living in the bogs are rich in the minerals that the soil lacks. So plants such as Venus's-flytrap and the pitcher plant catch and "eat" insects to get the minerals they need.

The leaves of the pitcher plant are shaped like deep vases, with insides that are slippery. Insects smell the nectar produced inside the plant and climb over the rim of the leaf. They soon slide down into a liquid and drown! Then the pitcher plant takes in, or absorbs, the minerals from the insect's body.

The hinged leaves of Venus's-flytrap lie open, waiting for an insect to pass by. When the insect touches the hairs on the fleshy part of the leaf, the two parts snap shut like a trap. Substances called enzymes ooze from the leaf and break down the insect's body so that the plant can absorb minerals from it.

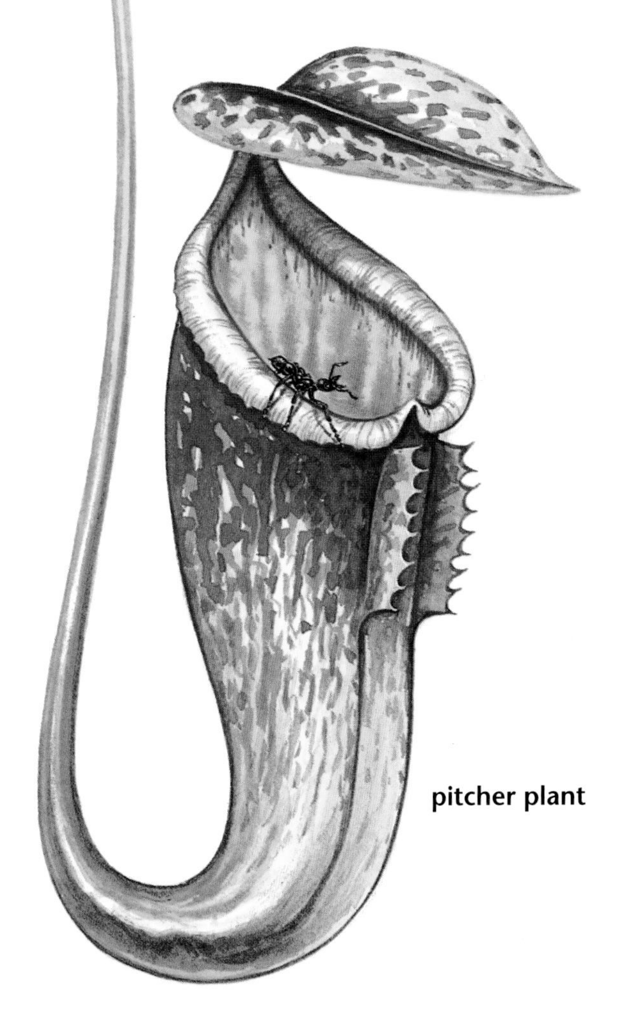

pitcher plant

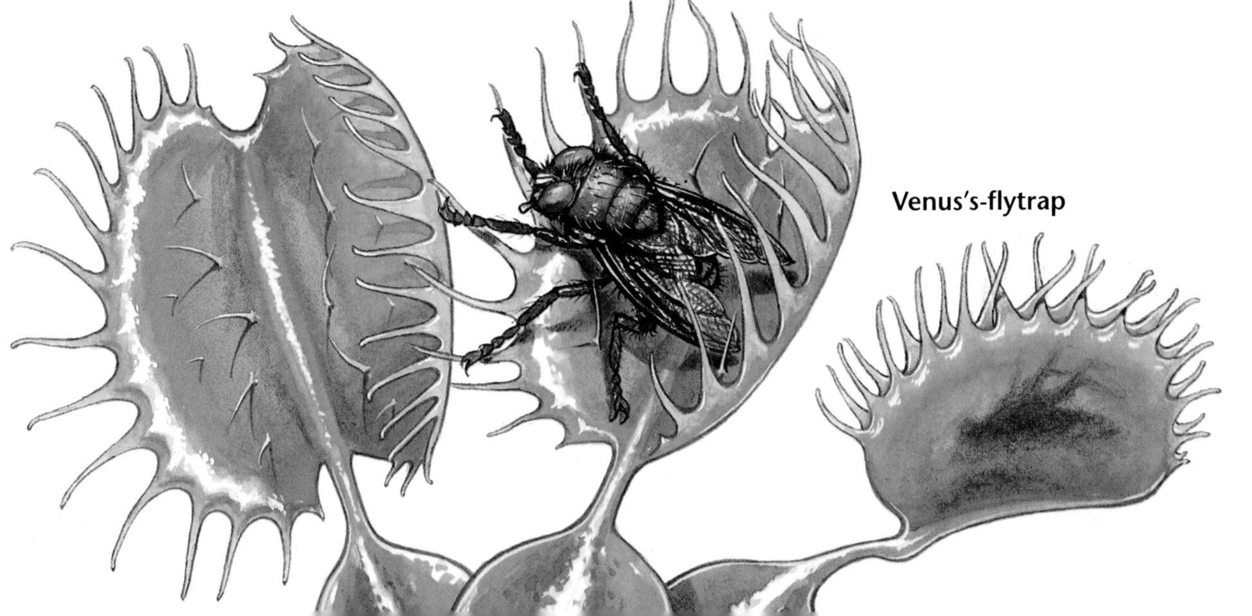

Venus's-flytrap

What do plants need to grow?

Do you have any plants growing in flowerpots around your home? Do you take care of them? How do you do this? You probably keep the plants in a place where sunlight can reach their leaves. And you probably water the soil regularly. Occasionally you might even add plant food to make sure your plants grow strong and healthy.

What do plants really need? Plants need sunlight and water. Plants also need minerals and nutrients to make them healthy. The soil in which the plants grow usually contains these minerals and nutrients.

Plants also need two gases from the air—**oxygen** and **carbon dioxide.** Plants breathe oxygen in and out. They use carbon dioxide from the atmosphere to help them make their food. There is also air in the soil, which plants don't take in but which they do need for healthy growth.

Both indoor and outdoor plants need sunlight, water, air, minerals, and nutrients to grow strong and healthy.

How much air is in the soil?

You will need:

water

a large spoon

a large measuring cup

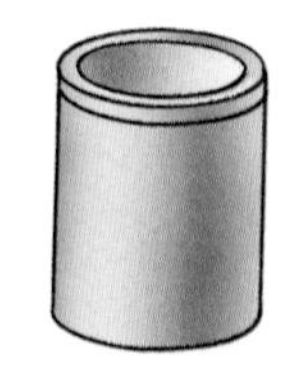

a small aluminum can

1. Fill the can right to the top with water and pour the water into the measuring cup. This will tell you exactly how much water was in the can.

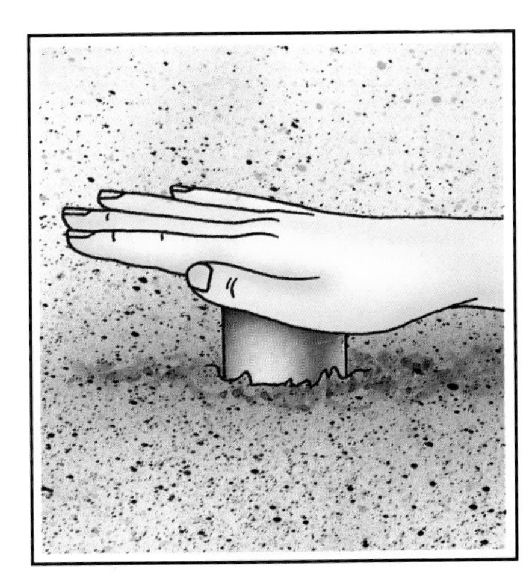

2. Take the can to a place such as a garden where there is soil. Push the can upside down into the ground until the bottom of the can is level with the top of the soil. You might have to push the can down with your foot.

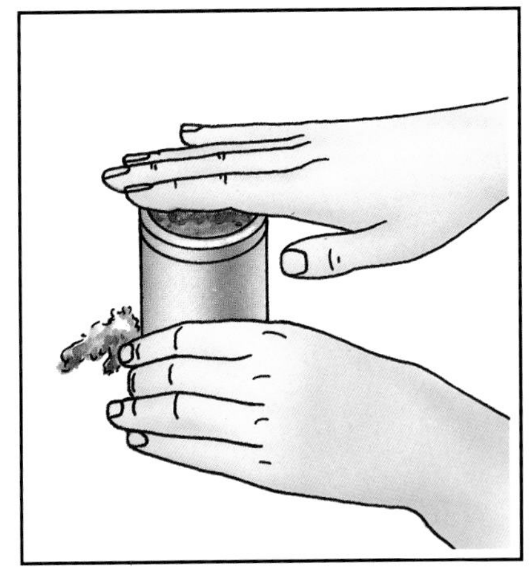

3. Now carefully ease the can out of the soil and smooth the surface of the soil so that it's level with the top of the can. You have now filled the same amount of space with soil as you did with water. Another way of saying this is that you have the same **volume** of soil as water.

4. Empty the soil into the water in the jug and stir it. You have put together a can of water and a can of soil. Do the soil and water now fill twice as much space? Can you explain your answer?

5. Can you figure out how much air was in the can of dirt? Explain how you can do this.

Try this experiment with different kinds of soil. Do they all contain the same amount of air?

All plants need sunlight

What color are lettuce leaves? What color are the needles of a pine tree? What color are the leaves of grasses and most garden plants? The leaves of all these plants are green. Do you know why?

Unlike animals that have to eat green plants or other living things to stay alive, plants are able to make their own food. All living things are made up of **cells,** but plant cells are different from animal cells. The cells in the leaves of most plants contain tiny green parts called **chloroplasts.** Each chloroplast contains the chemical called chlorophyll that makes the leaves green. The chloroplasts use sunlight, carbon dioxide and water to make food for the plant.

How do plants make their food?

The process by which a plant makes its own food using sunlight, water, and carbon dioxide is called **photosynthesis.** Sunlight shines into a leaf through its outer cells, which are clear like glass. The water comes from the soil, through the roots and the stem, and into the leaf. The air gets into the leaf through tiny holes called **stomata.** Inside the leaf, the chloroplasts use the sunlight as energy. This energy helps to make sugars by combining water with the carbon dioxide that's found in the air. The sugars are then turned into a substance called **starch.** Grains of starch are stored in the cells of the leaf until the plant needs them for food.

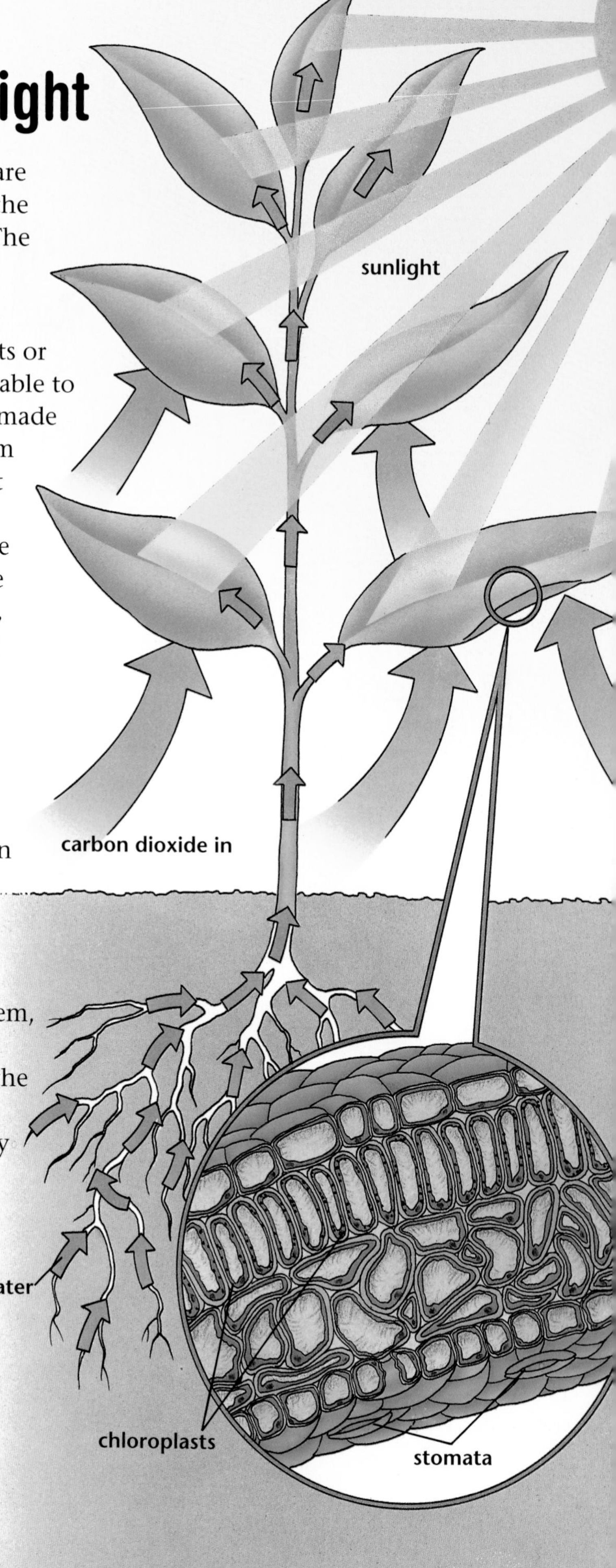

During the process called photosynthesis, the chloroplasts inside the leaves of a plant use sunlight, carbon dioxide, and water to make food.

Mushrooms are not green!

Did you ever wonder why mushrooms, which look somewhat like plants, are not green? Mushrooms and other fungi have no green parts, because their cells do not contain any chloroplasts. Botanists do not classify fungi as plants. Fungi belong to a separate kingdom of living things called **Fungi.**

This pink fungus is growing in a forest in Australia. Fungi usually use decaying animal and plant material to survive.

What happens to seedlings in the dark?

You will need:

two small damp cloths

two saucers

some mustard seeds

1. Cover each saucer with a damp cloth and scatter some mustard seeds over the cloths.

2. Put one saucer in a light place, such as on a window sill. Put the other saucer in a dark place, such as a cupboard or a large cookie tin with a lid.

3. Check once a day to make sure the cloths are damp, but not soaking wet. Try not to let the light into the dark place for any longer than a few seconds. Keep a record of your observations.

The seedlings in the light grow green and straight. But the seedlings in the dark grow weak and yellow. All the seeds had just enough food and water inside them to start growing. But plants need light to make more food. Without light, plants lose their greenness and will soon die.

What's in the soil?

Almost all the land on our planet is covered by a layer of **soil.** Do you know what's in the soil? Soil is a mixture of living and non-living material. It includes the rotting remains of plants and animals, tiny living things, air, water, and small bits of rock.

Look at a sample of soil through a magnifying glass or under a microscope, and you'll often see that it's full of living things. Some of these living things are small invertebrate animals, such as worms and insects. Others are bacteria and molds—but you won't see them. These living things help to create a part of the soil that's called **humus.**

Humus is the **organic** part of the soil, which means that it is made of material that was once alive. Most of the humus is made from the leaves, stems, and flowers of dead plants. The bacteria, molds, and invertebrates in the soil feed on this dead and decaying plant material. The waste material which these organisms leave behind is full of nutrients that provide food for living plants to grow. Humus also holds air and water in the soil.

The rest of the soil is made up of particles of rocks. The big particles are sand and the smallest ones are clay. Because rocks are not living things, we say that they are **inorganic.** Soil is a mixture of organic and inorganic materials.

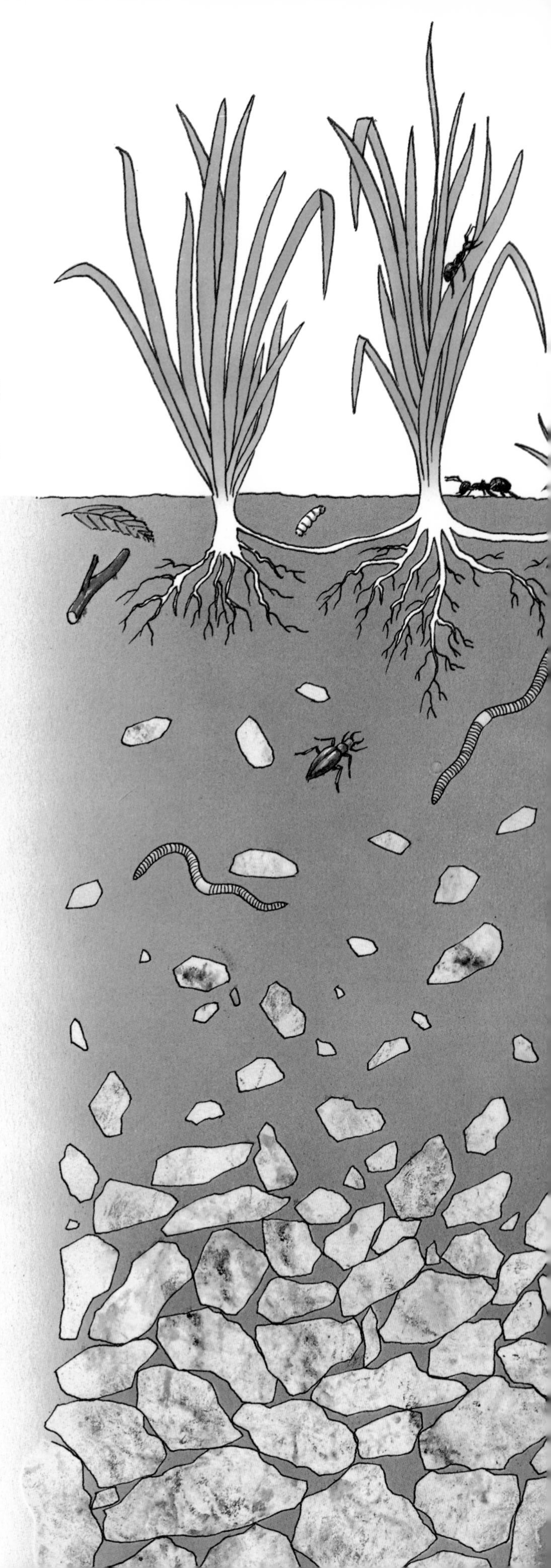

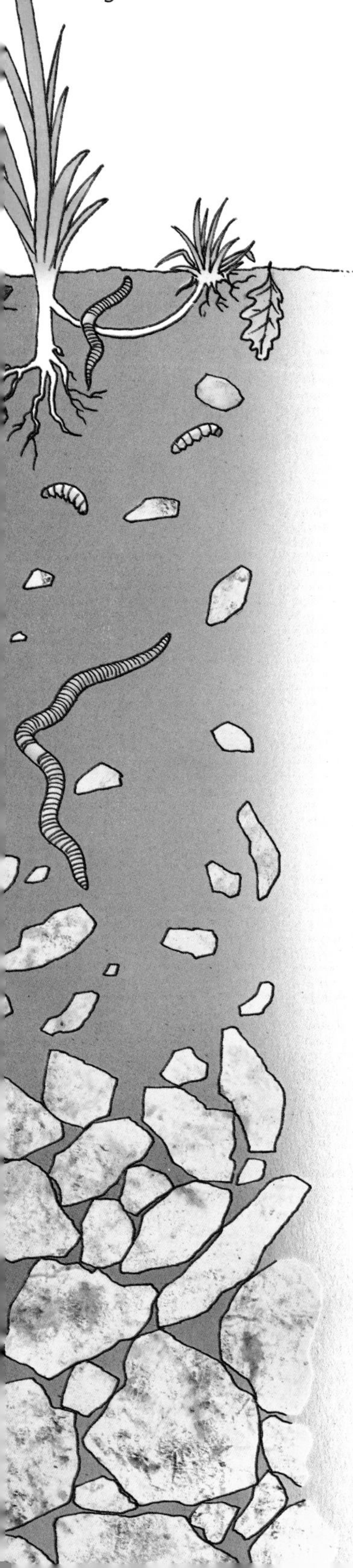

The upper layer of the soil contains lots of rotting organic material. The lower layers consist almost entirely of inorganic material.

What is soil made of?

You will need:

a handful of garden soil or forest floor soil

water

a small stick

a small glass jar

1. Half fill a glass jar with water and then put in a handful of soil.

2. Use the stick to stir the soil into the water. Then leave it to settle.

3. Watch as the soil settles in different layers. What falls to the bottom of the jar first? What settles above that? And what settles as the top layer?

Even if you wait a long time, the water will never become completely clear because some of the smallest pieces of clay will remain floating in it. Bits of plants and leaves will stay floating on the surface.

Try this experiment with soil from different places. Are the different layers in the jar always the same thickness?

Roots, stems, and leaves

When you look out your window, how many different kinds of plants do you see? Are there trees, shrubs, vines, or flowers? These are all plants. Do you have a lawn? That's a plant, too!

All these plants may look different, but they have a lot in common. Most plants have roots, a stem, and leaves. Inside the roots, stems, and leaves are special kinds of tubes called **vascular tissue.** This network of tiny tubes through a plant's body is called its **vascular system.** Most plants you see have a vascular system, and so they are called **vascular plants.**

The vascular system has a very important job to do. Water enters a plant through its roots and then travels through the tiny tubes in the stem to even smaller tubes in the leaves. This process is called **absorption.**

Some of this water is used up when the plant makes its food. Most water is needed to prevent the plant from wilting, but some comes out of the plant through hundreds of small holes in the leaves called **stomata.** This process is called **transpiration.**

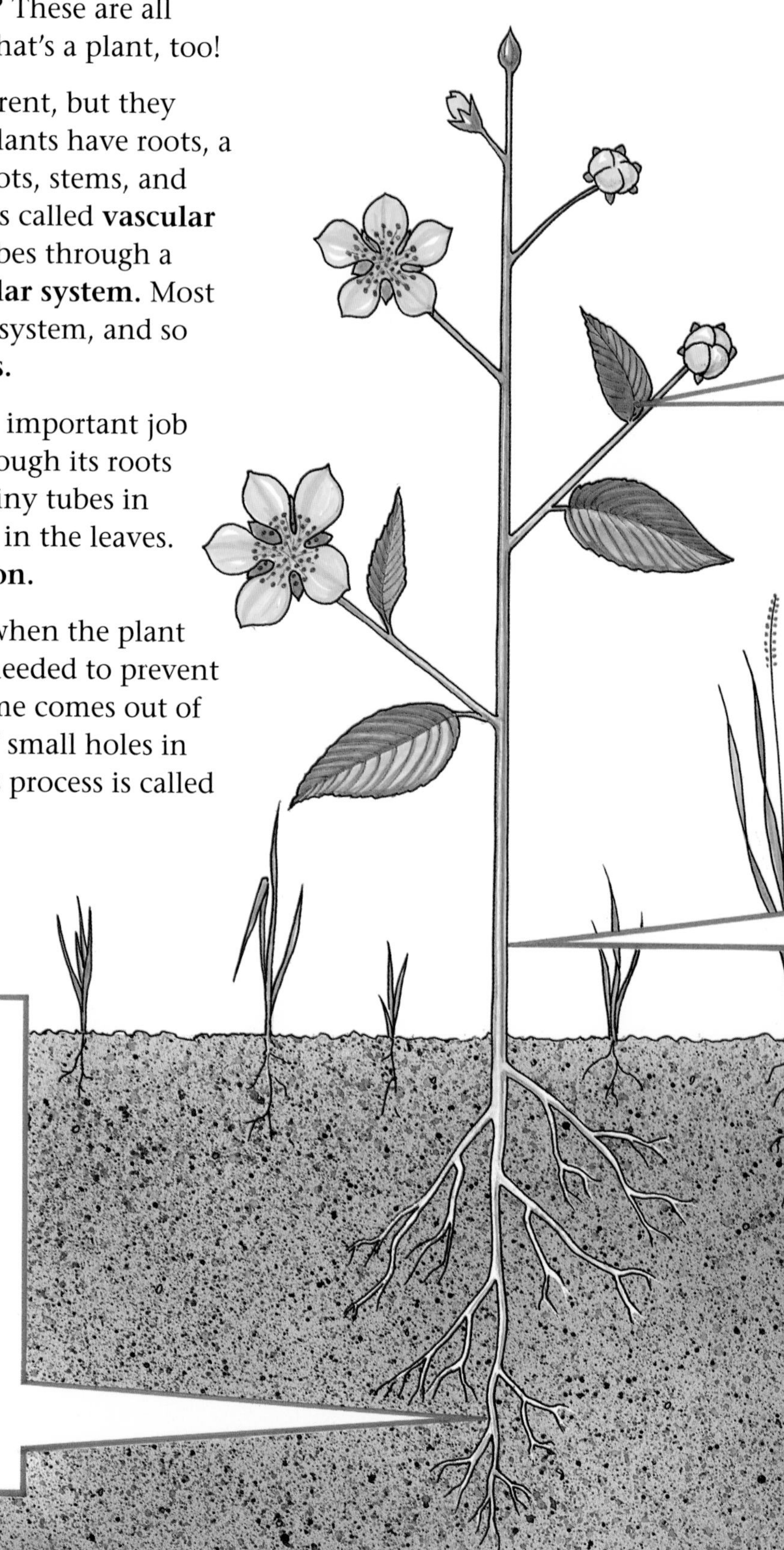

The roots

The roots of a plant fix it firmly in the soil where it grows. Some roots are thick and strong, but others are as thin and delicate as hairs. The thin roots take up water from the soil. The water contains tiny amounts of substances called minerals and nutrients that help the plants to grow strong and healthy.

The leaves

The leaves are the food-making factories of a plant. Inside each leaf there's a green chemical called **chlorophyll.** Chlorophyll allows the plant to use energy from sunlight to make food. Botanists call this process **photosynthesis.**

The stem

The tubes that carry water up the stems of tall plants are very strong. The stem is like a flagpole, holding up the leaves and flowers above the soil so that they can get plenty of sunlight. This is very important because plants use sunlight to help them make most of their own food.

Make a rainbow salad

You will need:

red, blue, yellow, green, and orange food coloring

water

five small jars

five fresh celery stalks

1. Put about 1 inch (2.5 centimeters) of water in each jar. Add a few drops of coloring, red in one jar, blue in the next, and so on.

2. Put a stalk of celery in each jar, with the thicker end in the water. Leave the jars for two hours. When you come back, describe what has happened.

Find out more by looking at pages **106–107**

Plants with spores

Do you go out walking in the woods? Around damp, shady woodland or bushes, on the ground, trees, rocks, and walls, you can often see patches of bright green that are soft to touch. These are green plants called **mosses.** Mosses grow best in damp places, though many types can survive for some time in dry weather. Even if they have dried up and turned brown, plenty of water will soon make them green again.

Most mosses are less than 6 inches (15 centimeters) tall. These mosses can't grow any taller because they don't have a vascular system to carry food and water from one part of the plant to another. Instead, they absorb water and other nutrients through tiny hairs called **rhizoids.** The rhizoids also anchor the plants to the ground.

Because mosses have no vascular system, they are called **nonvascular plants.** Along with liverworts and hornworts, they belong to a special group of plants called **bryophytes.** Bryophytes don't have true leaves, stems, and roots. Botanists think that they may have been the very first land plants.

Next time you go to the woods, take a magnifying glass with you and take a close look at some moss. You'll see lots of thin stems covered with tiny green leaves. On the bottom of the moss you'll see the rhizoids that hold the moss down on the ground. On the thin stalks above the leaves, you might see some tiny, podlike capsules. Inside these capsules are the spores that are carried by the wind to make new moss plants.

Liverworts are bryophytes that also grow very close to the ground. They often measure less than 1/2 inch (1.4 centimeters) high. Liverworts grow in damp, shady places and are sometimes found in water.

Tree ferns in Australia and New Zealand grow stems like large trunks. They can be as high as 83 feet (25 meters), with the fronds at the top.

How do ferns grow?

Ferns are plants that grow in damp and shady places. All ferns reproduce by using spores. Ferns can grow taller than mosses because they have a vascular system. This system is made up of tiny tubes inside their stems and leaves. These tubes carry food and water from one part of the plant to another. The stems of many ferns grow underground, so the large leaves, called **fronds**, seem to grow straight up out of the ground. Each frond is divided into lots of smaller leaflets.

Releasing spores

Fern spores grow in tiny clusters on the underside of the plant's leaves. These clusters are made up of tiny pod-like receptacles, called **sporangia.** Each sporangium splits open and releases the spores, which then fall to the ground below.

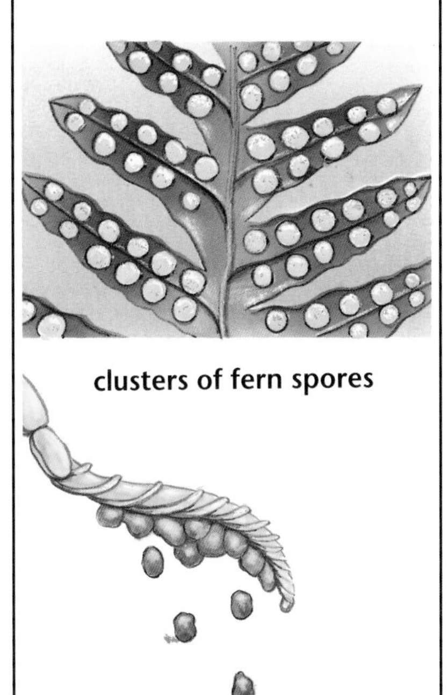

clusters of fern spores

sporangium releasing spores

Find out more by looking at pages **94–95**
96–97
98–99

Plants with seeds

Have you ever planted seeds in a garden? You can start a flower or vegetable garden with seeds. But trees and all sorts of other plants can also be grown from seeds.

Plants that grow from seeds are called **seed-bearing plants** or **seed plants.** There are so many kinds of seed plants that botanists divide them into two smaller groups.

The seed pod of the common corn poppy contains hundreds of tiny seeds that are scattered by the wind. Each seed can grow into a mature poppy plant.

Flowering plants

The first group is called **angiosperms.** Angiosperms are flowering plants. They produce seeds that are enclosed in the protective seed case called the **ovary.**

Garden plants like roses, daisies, and sunflowers are angiosperms. So are vegetables, herbs, and the grains that we eat. All plants that produce fruit and flowers are angiosperms—that's almost all the plants in the world!

Most trees and shrubs are angiosperms, too. But not all of them!

Gymnosperms

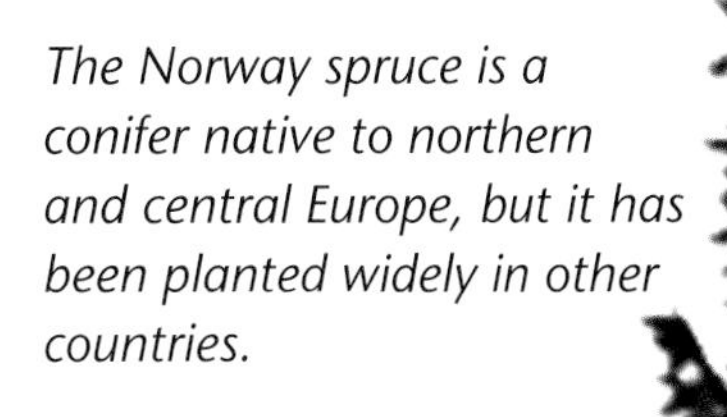

The Norway spruce is a conifer native to northern and central Europe, but it has been planted widely in other countries.

Some trees and shrubs belong to the second group of seed plants called **gymnosperms.** Most gymnosperms produce naked or uncovered seeds in a cone, and they do not have flowers. **Conifers,** such as pines, firs, spruces, and balsams, are gymnosperms.

There are other kinds of gymnosperms, too. **Cycads** live in the tropics, and they look like very large palm trees. Cycads are very old plants. They covered large parts of Earth during prehistoric times. Today, they grow in only a few small areas.

The **gingko** is also a gymnosperm, but it does not bear cones. It is a large tree with fan-shaped leaves that bears seeds at the ends of its branches. It is the only surviving species of a group of plants that lived millions of years ago.

Needles

Cone

Norway spruce

Cycad trees live only in warm, moist regions. They bear heavy cones that may grow 3 feet (91 centimeters) long.

The Ginko tree is a single species. It bears seeds but not fruits or cones.

Making new plants

Have you ever tried to grow your own plants? If you have, you may have started with seeds. Plants have male and female parts. In seed-bearing plants, the male reproductive cells, called **sperm**, are carried in tiny grains called **pollen.** These cells are released into the **ovary**, the female part of the plant. There, one of the sperm joins with a female reproductive cell, called an **egg**, to start a new plant. This tiny new plant, called an **embryo**, is at first kept in a seed with its own store of food.

Seeds can be many different shapes and sizes but they all do the same job. They are scattered away from the parent plant. The outer cover of each seed protects the embryo until the seed lands in a suitable place. When conditions are right, the seed takes up water and the new plant grows out of it. This is called **germination.**

*Most flowers, such as this mallow, have both male and female parts. The male parts are the stamens, each consisting of a stalk and an anther. The female parts consist of the ovary, the style, and the stigma. Flowers with both male and female parts are said to be **perfect.** If flowers have separate male and female parts, they are called **imperfect.** A few species even have separate "male" and "female" plants.*

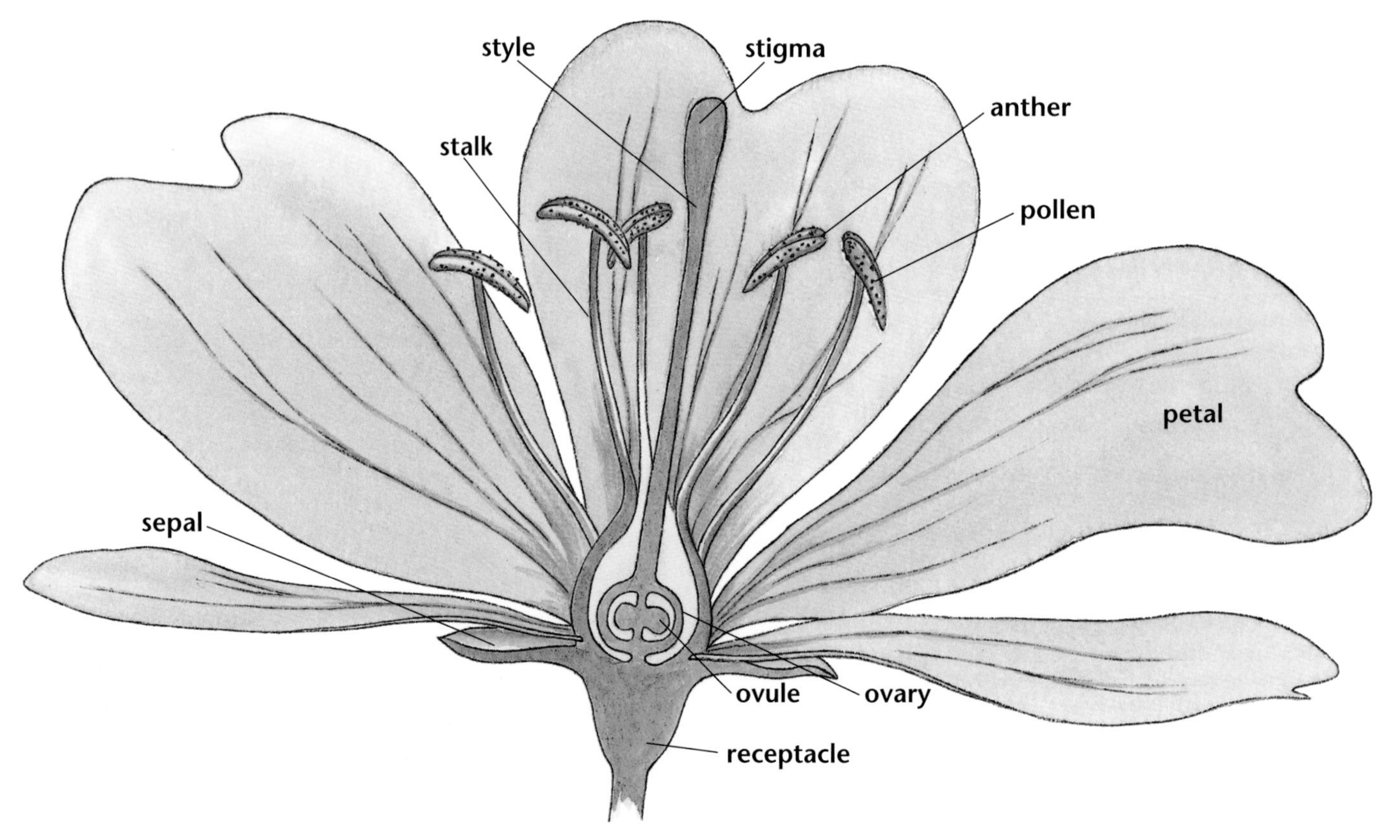

Flowers and more flowers

There are thousands of different kinds of flowers, many with beautiful shapes and colors. But flowers are not made just for us to look at and admire. Flowering plants need flowers to produce seeds so that more plants can grow.

Look closely at the drawing of the flower below. At the bottom of the flower is a green part called the **receptacle.**

Now look inside the petals. In the center of the flower is the ovary, which is the female part. It contains the **ovules,** which will become seeds. The ovary has one or more stalklike **styles** with sticky tops, or **stigmas.** Between the ovary and the petals are the male parts, or **stamens.** Each stamen has a stalk, at the top of which is an **anther.** Pollen grains, which carry the male cells, are produced in the anthers. Try looking at several different flowers, and see if you can find the parts that make new seeds.

In the hibiscus flower, the yellow pollen-covered stamens are held apart from the red stigma.

New plants from cones

Cone-bearing plants reproduce in a way that's a bit different from flowering plants. Plants that make their seeds in cones have two different kinds of cones on each plant. The male cone produces the pollen, and the female cone produces the ovules.

Both male and female cones are made up of many scales arranged around a central axis. In the female cone, the scales are thick and woody. Each scale carries two ovules, which will become seeds. Male cones are smaller and softer than female cones. They have pollen sacs on their scales, in which pollen grains are produced.

The life of a cone

1. The small male cones are produced in groups at the ends of twigs. They produce yellow pollen. You will see clouds of pollen if you shake a branch during the hot months of the year.

2. The young female cones are produced upright and singly at the ends of the shoots. At first they are pink, but later they become green and turn downward.

3. Pollen grains get between the scales of young female cones and carry male cells directly onto the ovules.

Find out more by looking at pages **92–93**
98–99

Making fertile seeds

The wind carries the pollen grains, and some of them land between the scales of female cones. The pollen grains stick to a sticky substance near the ovules. Pollen then enters the pollen chamber of the ovule, where a mature seed will grow in one to two years.

After the seed is released, tiny wings cause it to twirl and float in the wind. If a seed lands in the right place, it will grow into a new plant.

4. The seeds take one to two years to mature and then they are released.

5. Cones usually open their scales to let the seeds out. Some types of cones fall apart to release their seeds.

6. The seeds have small wings and are easily carried away by the wind.

7. In dry weather, the scales of a cone open and the seeds blow away. When it rains, the scales close up again. Rain will wash the seeds down onto the ground.

Find out more by looking at pages **78–79**
92–93
96–97

What is pollination?

Have you ever noticed how pleasant many flowers smell? They have attractive scents, as well as bright colors, in order to draw insects. Insects use the nectar made by flowers as food. In the process of getting the food, the insects transfer pollen from flower to flower.

The process of seed formation begins with this transfer of pollen grains from one flower to the stigma of another flower of the same kind. This transfer is called **pollination.** The main insects which pollinate flowers are bees and butterflies. These insects feed on the sweet liquid called **nectar** that is usually produced by special cells in the flower's receptacle.

Bees feed on pollen as well as on nectar. They carry the pollen back to their nests in small pollen "baskets" on their back legs.

Some flowers are pollinated by birds and small mammals. In its search for nectar, this honey possum is pollinating a eucalyptus flower.

On its way to the nectar, the insect has to pass the flower's anthers, which are covered in pollen. Some of the pollen sticks to the insect's body and then brushes off onto the stigma of the next flower that the insect visits. A thin tube grows from the pollen grain, down through the style, and into the ovule. A male cell, carried by this pollen tube, unites with an egg, and the ovule starts to develop into a fertile seed.

Wind pollination

Some flowering plants, such as grasses and hazel trees, don't have any nectar in their flowers to attract insects. These plants need the wind to pollinate them. The wind blows the pollen off the anthers of one flower and onto the sticky stigma of another flower. The stigma of a wind-pollinated plant can be large and feathery, in order to catch the pollen more easily. The wind takes the pollen from male cones to the ovules of female pine cones.

Seeds and fruits

Do you like to grow flowers and vegetables? You can make a garden just about anywhere. Maybe you have a vegetable patch in your backyard. Lots of people put shrubs and flowers in their front yard. If you don't have much room, you can even grow flowers and herbs in containers indoors, or in window boxes.

No matter where you plant your garden, you can start it with seeds. Soon you'll have beautiful flowers to pick for a bouquet, or delicious herbs and vegetables to eat. You can pick whatever you'd like to grow, as long as the plant can live in your climate.

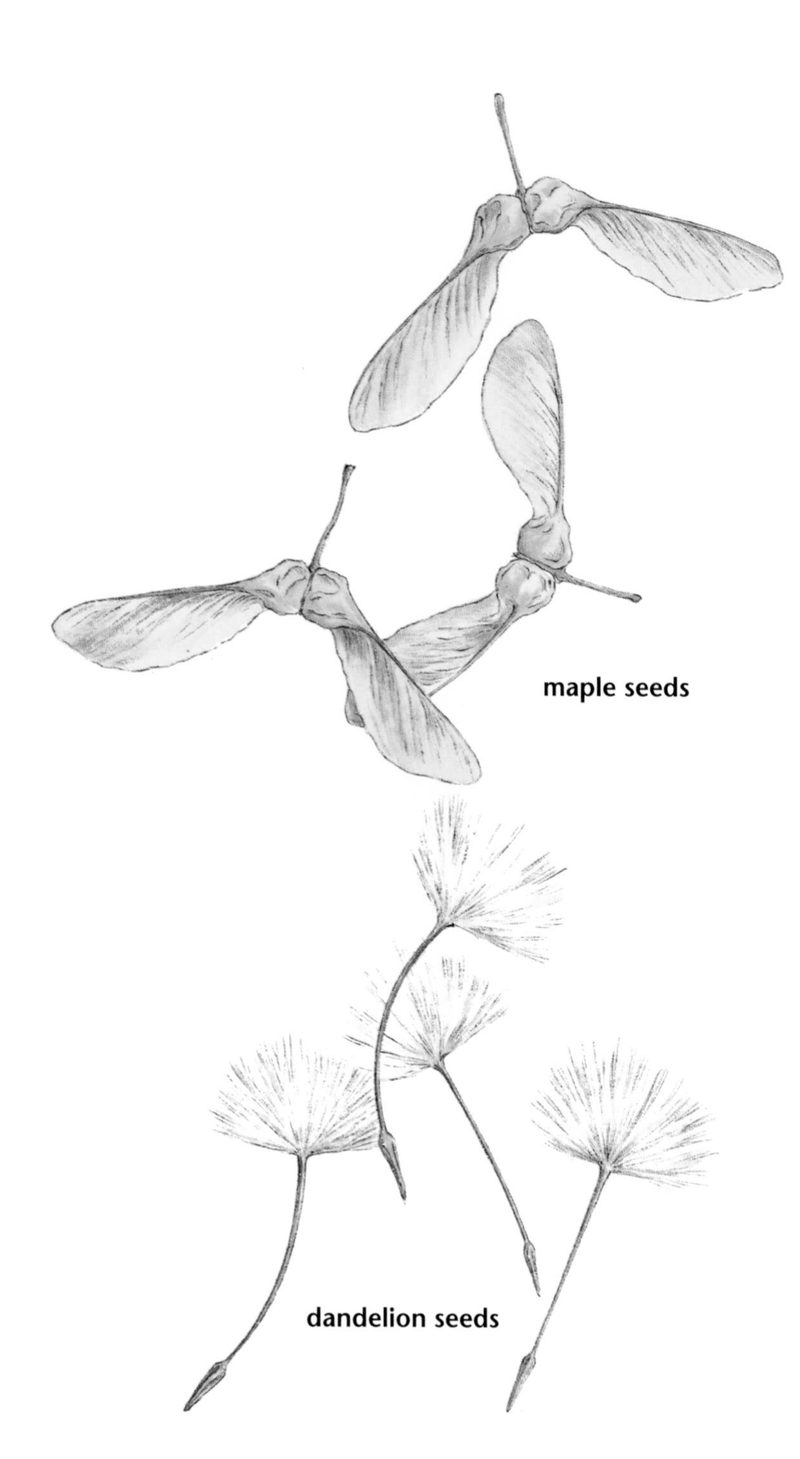

Find the right place to grow

When we grow plants in our gardens, we carefully choose places for the seeds. In the wild, this is left to chance. Seeds need to spread far away from the plant that produced them. If the seeds don't move away, they can't grow properly. The parent plant might shade them from the sunlight they need and take up most of the water and nutrients from that area of the soil.

How do seeds move away from parent plants? Some seeds are scattered by the wind. Maple and elm seeds have wings to help them fly away. Other seeds, such as those of dandelion and milkweed, have fine hairs that help the wind carry them away.

Helping the seeds

Animals help carry some of the seeds that are found inside fruits. The animal eats the fruit with the seeds inside it. The seeds go right through the animal's stomach without being digested. The seeds then pass out of the animal along with its waste matter.

The fruits of burs and cleavers are covered in tiny hooks that get caught on animal fur or human clothes. Sometimes these fruits are carried a long way before they fall off.

The fruits of some plants scatter their seeds by exploding! The seed pods of beans and balsams dry out and suddenly break open, scattering the seeds all around.

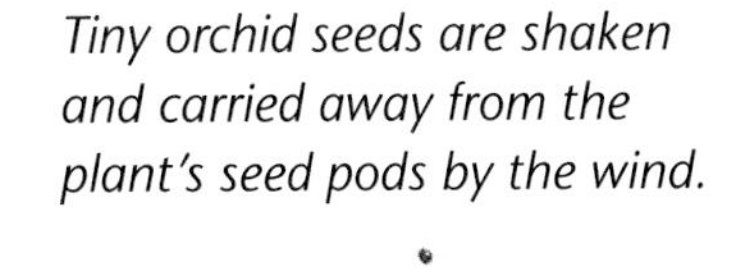

Tiny orchid seeds are shaken and carried away from the plant's seed pods by the wind.

Burs, the seedcases of the cocklebur plant, usually contain two seeds each. When a mammal passes the plant, some burs stick to its fur or hair.

Birds disperse the seeds of plants that have brightly colored berries. They eat the berries and deposit the seeds as waste.

Find out more by looking at pages **84–85**
94–95
104–105

How do seeds germinate?

The name for the moment in which seeds start to grow is **germination.** Seeds come in many different shapes and sizes—big ones, small ones, round ones, flat ones, and thin ones. No matter what they look like, each seed has a tough outer coat and enough stored food to start growing.

Some seeds can wait a long time before they germinate. If you buy a packet of seeds and keep it dry, you can plant the seeds several years later and they will still grow into healthy plants. Some poppy and dock seeds have stayed underground for many years before germinating into new plants!

When a seed germinates, one part grows upward and one part grows downward. The part that grows upward is called a **shoot,** and the part that grows downward is called a **root.**

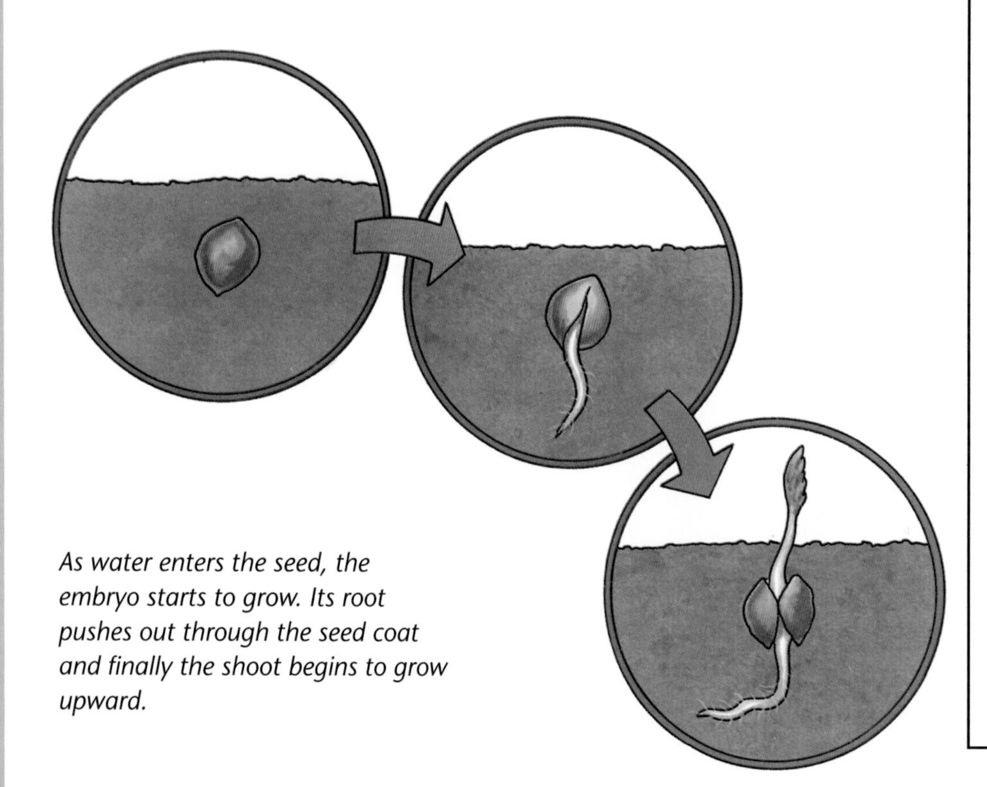

As water enters the seed, the embryo starts to grow. Its root pushes out through the seed coat and finally the shoot begins to grow upward.

You will need:

self-adhesive labels

a felt-tipped pen

eight paper tissues

a small spoon

a packet of seeds, such as grass, mustard, or lettuce

four small jars with tight-fitting lids

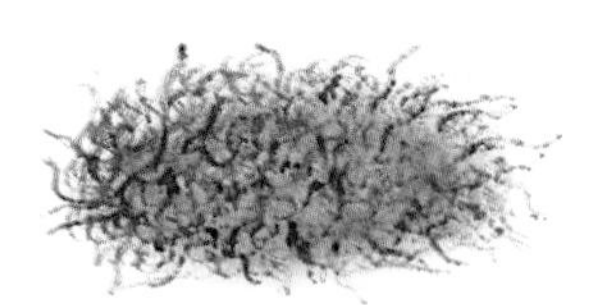

some moist steel wool

What do seeds need to germinate?

Seeds will not germinate until they receive three things—water, warmth, and oxygen—all at the same time and in the correct amounts. You can prove this for yourself by carrying out a simple experiment.

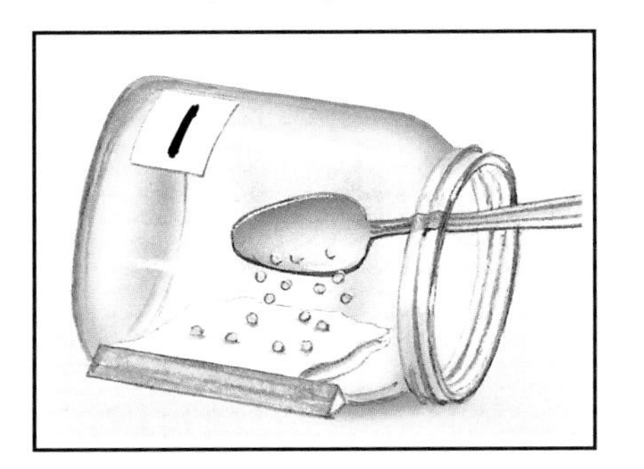

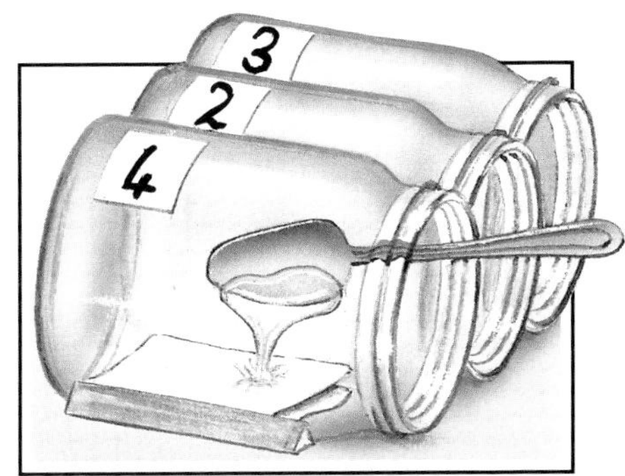

1. Number your jars, 1, 2, 3, and 4. Lay the jars on their sides. Put two paper tissues into each jar. Use the spoon to sprinkle some seeds into jar 1. Screw on the lid.

2. Put a little water into the other three jars to make the tissues damp, but not soaking wet.

3. Sprinkle some seeds on the damp tissues. Screw on the lids of jars 2 and 3. Put the steel wool into jar 4, and screw on the lid.

4. Put jars 1, 3, and 4 in a kitchen cabinet. Put jar 2 in the refrigerator.

5. Look at your jars every two or three days, and keep a record of what happens to the seeds. Which ones are germinating? Which ones are not? Why? Are all the jars getting equal amounts of water, warmth, and oxygen? After about a week, check your findings against those printed below.

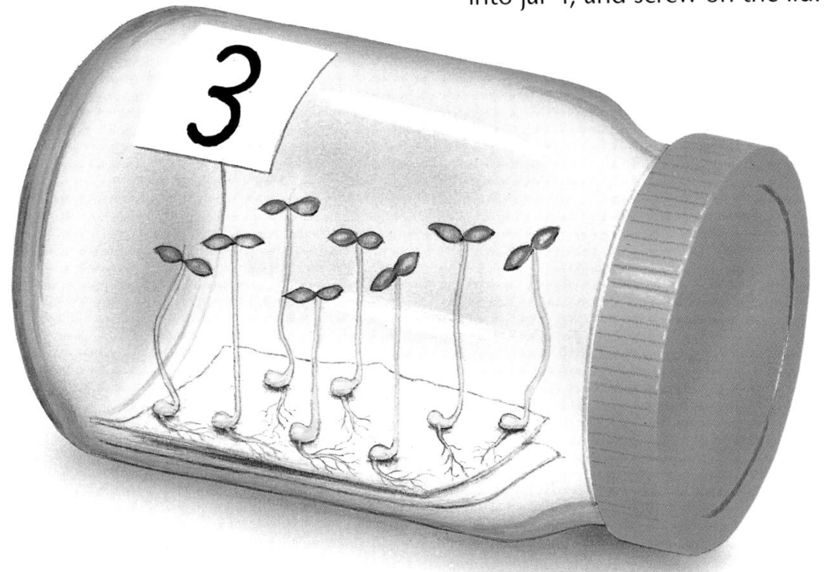

The seeds in jar number 3 should have sprouted into tall, thin seedlings. So we know that the conditions were right in jar 3. But none of the other seeds has germinated—the conditions were wrong in jars 1, 2, and 4. What were the three things that made the conditions right for the seeds in jar 3?

The seeds in jar 3 had warmth, water, and oxygen from the air. Jar 1 had warmth and oxygen, but no water. Jar 2 had oxygen and water but no warmth. Jar 4 had water and warmth, but no oxygen. The steel wool used up all the oxygen as it rusted. If you take the steel wool out, the seeds will soon grow.

Did you notice that the seeds don't need sunlight to germinate? All your seeds started to grow in the dark. Each seed has its own food supply with which to start, but when the plant grows bigger, it will also need sunlight to help it make more food.

Find out more by looking at pages **84–85**
102–103

Shoots and roots

Did you know that shoots grow upward? Shoots grow toward the light, which they need in order to make their own food. Sunlight provides the energy that plants use to make the sugars and starches that are their food.

Did you know that roots grow downward? Roots fix plants firmly in the ground. Large trees, for example, have many big, spreading roots to anchor them. Roots also absorb water and other nutrients to help plants grow.

Shoots and light

You will need:

some soil or potting compost

aluminum foil

water

a small flowerpot

some sweet corn seeds

1. Fill the flowerpot with the soil or potting compost. Sow your seeds in the soil, about 1/2 inch (1.25 centimeters) deep.

Keep the pot in a warm, dark place and make sure the soil is damp, but not soaking wet.

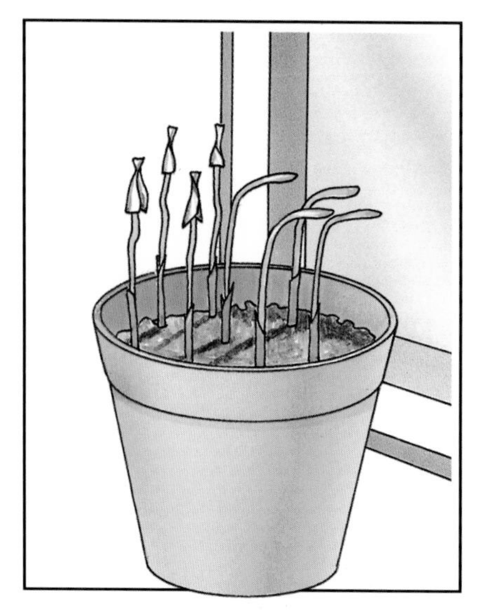

2. After a few days, when the shoots are about 1 inch (2.5 centimeters) high, put the pot on a window sill during the day. Cut out some small pieces of aluminum foil and twist them into tiny cones. Place the cones over the tips of half of the shoots in the pot, and leave the pot for an hour or two.

What has happened? Are the shoots all growing in the same direction? Can you explain what you see?

Roots grow down and shoots grow up

You can find out more about how roots and shoots grow by doing this simple experiment.

You will need:

pea or kidney bean seeds

some blotting paper or paper towels

water

a glass jar

1. Soak the seeds in water for a few hours. Pour some water into the jar —the water should be about 1/2 inch (1.25 centimeters) deep. Dampen the blotting paper or paper towels.

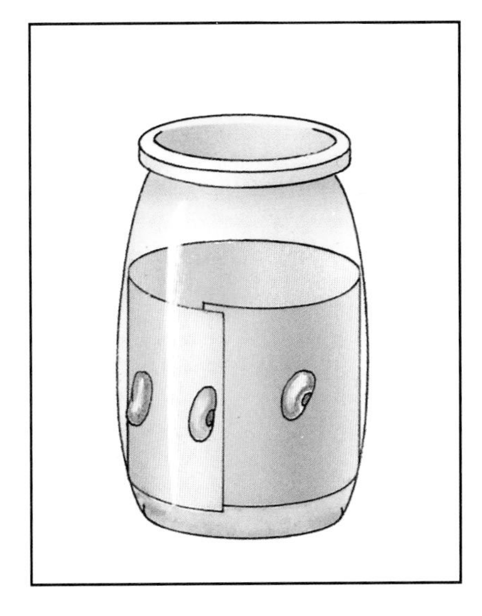

2. Arrange the seeds between the blotting paper or towels and the side of the jar, as shown.

3. Put the jar in a warm place. Always keep about 1/2 inch (1.25 centimeters) of water in it.

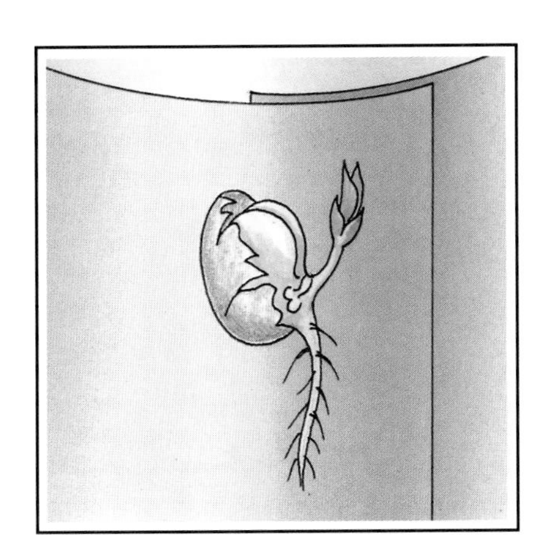

4. The root from each seed will burst through the coat in a few days. In what direction is it growing? The shoot will appear a little later. In what direction is it growing?

5. Now turn the jar on its side so that the root and shoot of each seed are pointing sideways. Leave the jar on its side overnight. In the morning, what do you see?

New plants without seeds

Some plants can reproduce themselves without using seeds. Many of these plants have male and female parts, but they may not use them to make seeds or spores. Instead, new plants develop from special buds on the parent plant.

Both the shoot and the roots are growing from the eye of this sprouting potato tuber.

When a plant spreads in this way, it is called **vegetative propagation.** You can make a new plant from any part of a parent plant—a root, stem, leaf, or flower!

The part of the potato plant that we eat is called the **tuber.** Tubers are part of the stem that grows underground. If they are not dug up and eaten, the tubers will grow into new potato plants. Look closely at a potato and you'll see the small buds, called **eyes,** that grow into new plants.

Bryophyllum is called the good luck plant. Tiny new plants grow on the edges of its leaves. The new plants drop down to the ground, root themselves and start growing as separate plants.

Strawberry plants, with their delicious red fruits, also produce long stems. These stems are called **runners,** and they grow across the soil surface. New plants grow on the runners and put down roots to take in water and nutrients from the soil.

Find out more by looking at pages **90–91**

New plants without seeds

Mosses and ferns make copies of themselves from **spores.** Spores are single cells which are easily carried by the wind. Some can survive in hot and dry conditions and sprout only when conditions are favorable.

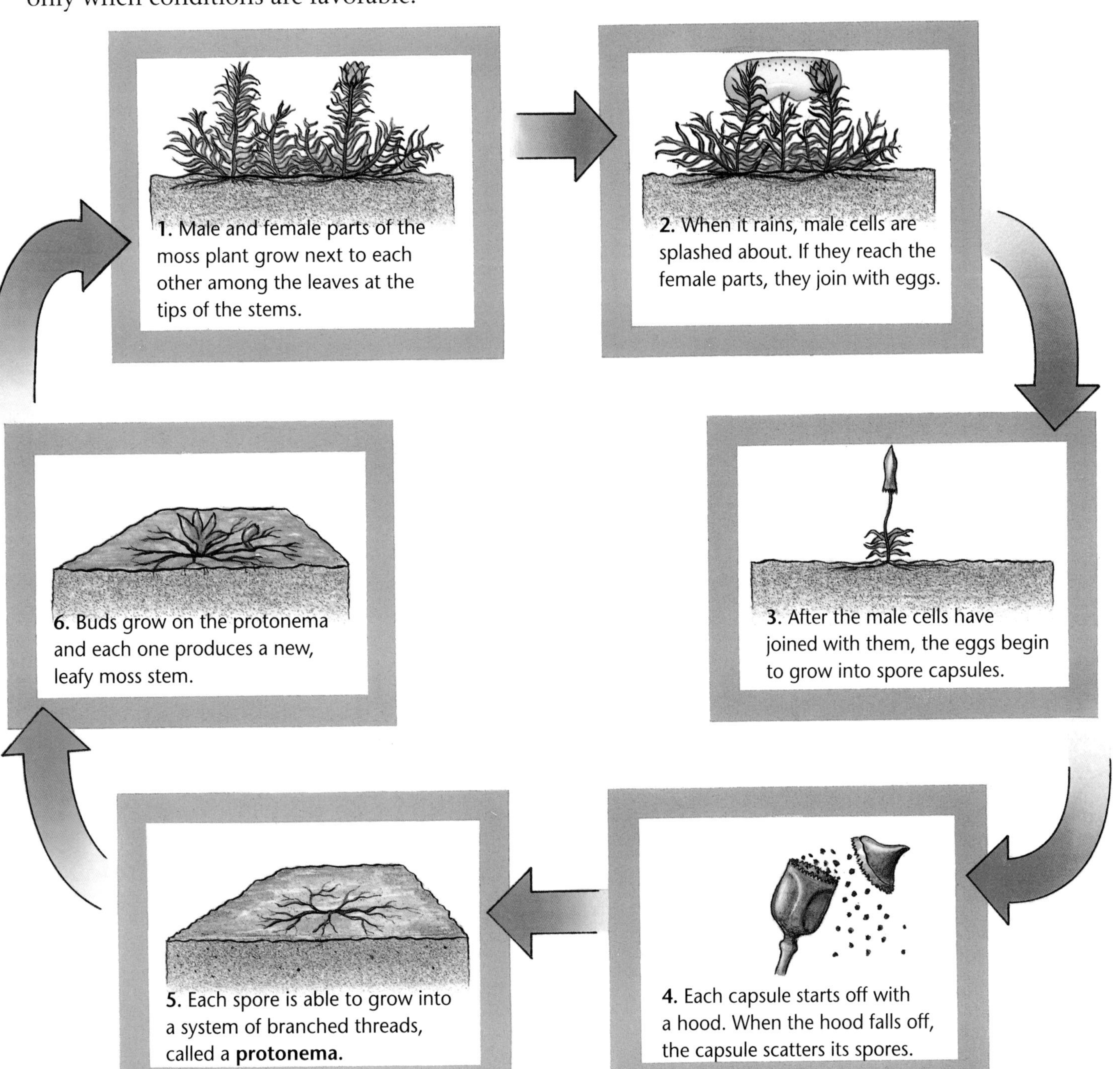

Plants in winter

Do you live in a cold climate? Then you may be wondering what happens to the flowers in winter. They seem to die off when the weather gets cold and snowy. Then, in spring, some flowering plants start growing again, bigger than ever. Others never come back. Why?

Some flowering plants, such as nasturtiums and giant sunflowers, start growing from seed in the spring, make beautiful flowers all summer, and then die when the weather gets cold. Because they grow and die all in one season, they have a very short life cycle. We call these plants **annuals.**

Other plants take two years to complete their life cycle. We call these plants **biennials.** In their first year, biennial plants store up food and become strong so they can survive over the winter. In their second year, they use the food they've stored up, flower, and then die. Flowers such as foxgloves, and vegetables such as carrots, parsnips, and rhubarb, are biennials. The herb parsley is also a biennial.

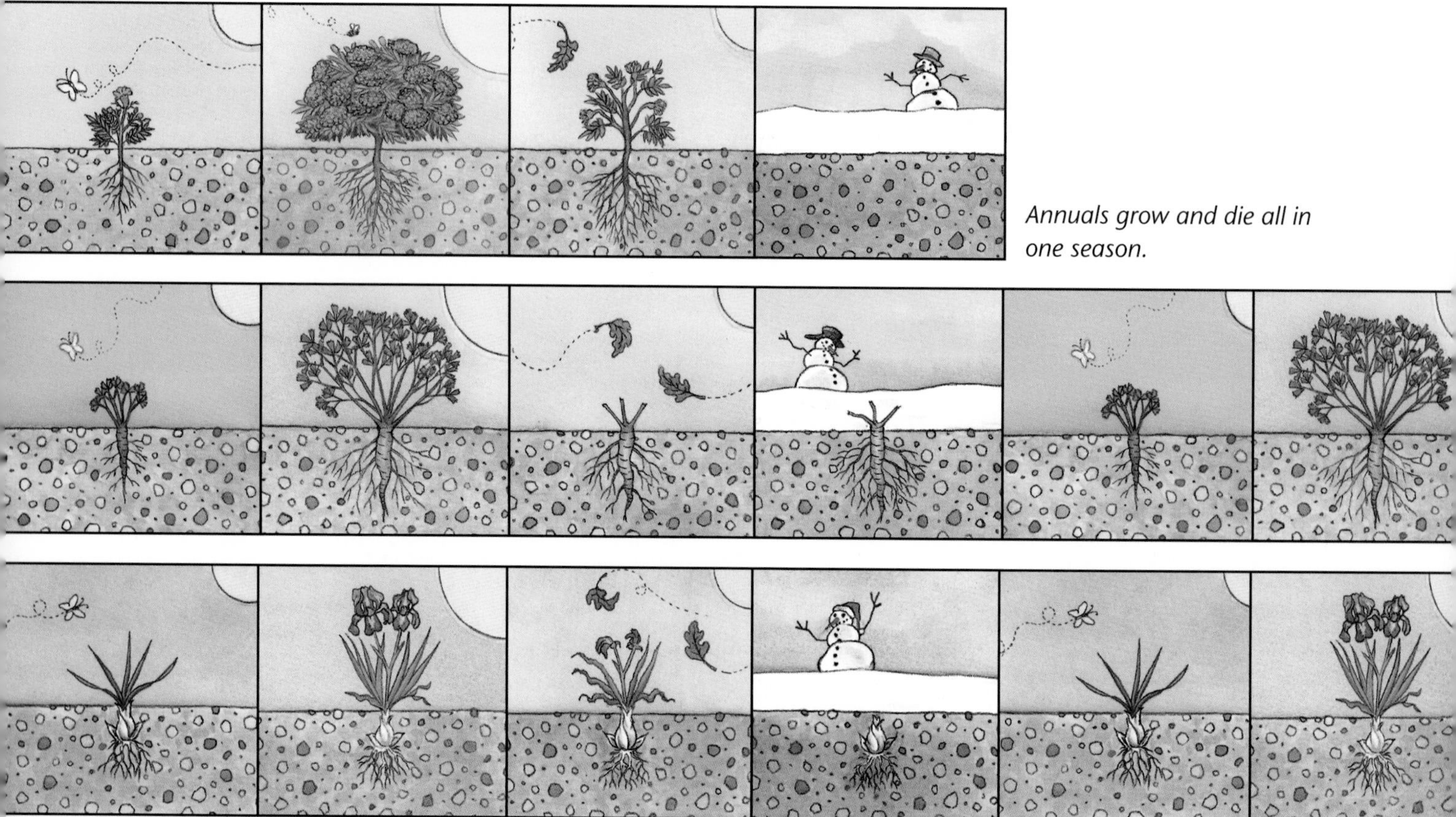

Annuals grow and die all in one season.

Find out more by looking at pages **72–73**
92–93

Year after year

Some plants can go on growing and flowering for many years. We call these plants **perennials.** Flowering plants such as irises, asters, and lilies are perennials. Shrubs and trees are perennials, too.

Some perennials seem to disappear in the winter. The parts aboveground die off when the weather gets cold. But the underground parts remain alive, and the plant produces new shoots in the spring when the weather warms up. These perennials are called **herbaceous perennials.**

Shrubs and trees are called **woody perennials.** They may lose their leaves in winter, but their bare stems can still be seen throughout the winter. Other woody perennials, such as pine trees and other conifers, remain green throughout the year.

a crocus in winter

Biennials take two years to complete their life cycle.

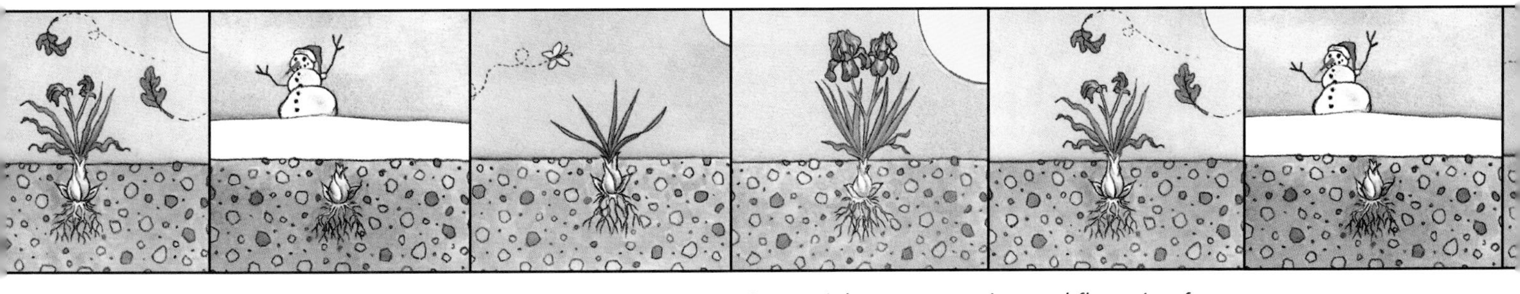

Perennials go on growing and flowering for many years.

Fruits, roots, and our food

How many plant products have you eaten today? Did you eat any bread, breakfast cereal, carrots, potatoes, cauliflower, lettuce, rice, apples, or peanuts? All over the world, people eat many different kinds of plant food.

The parts of a plant that we eat are usually those parts where the plant is storing its own supply of food. We eat different parts of different plants. Carrots are roots, lettuces and spinach are bunches of leaves, and cauliflower is a large head of flowers, which we eat before they open. Apples, pears, and oranges are some of the more popular fruits. **Fruit** is the part of a flowering plant that contains the plant's seeds. Therefore, nuts are fruit, as well as seeds. Eggplants, tomatoes, beans, and grains of wheat and rice are also fruits.

Think about what you eat

We can't eat every kind of plant. Some of the smaller ones contain nothing worth eating. Many others are too tough for us to digest. Many plants are poisonous or have poisonous parts. The leaves of potato plants, for example, are poisonous, but the potatoes that grow underground are good to eat.

Plants are obviously very important foods. Many people in the world eat nothing but food that comes from plants. We call these people **vegetarians.** Even people who eat meat depend on plants. Most of the animals that provide this meat have been fed on plants.

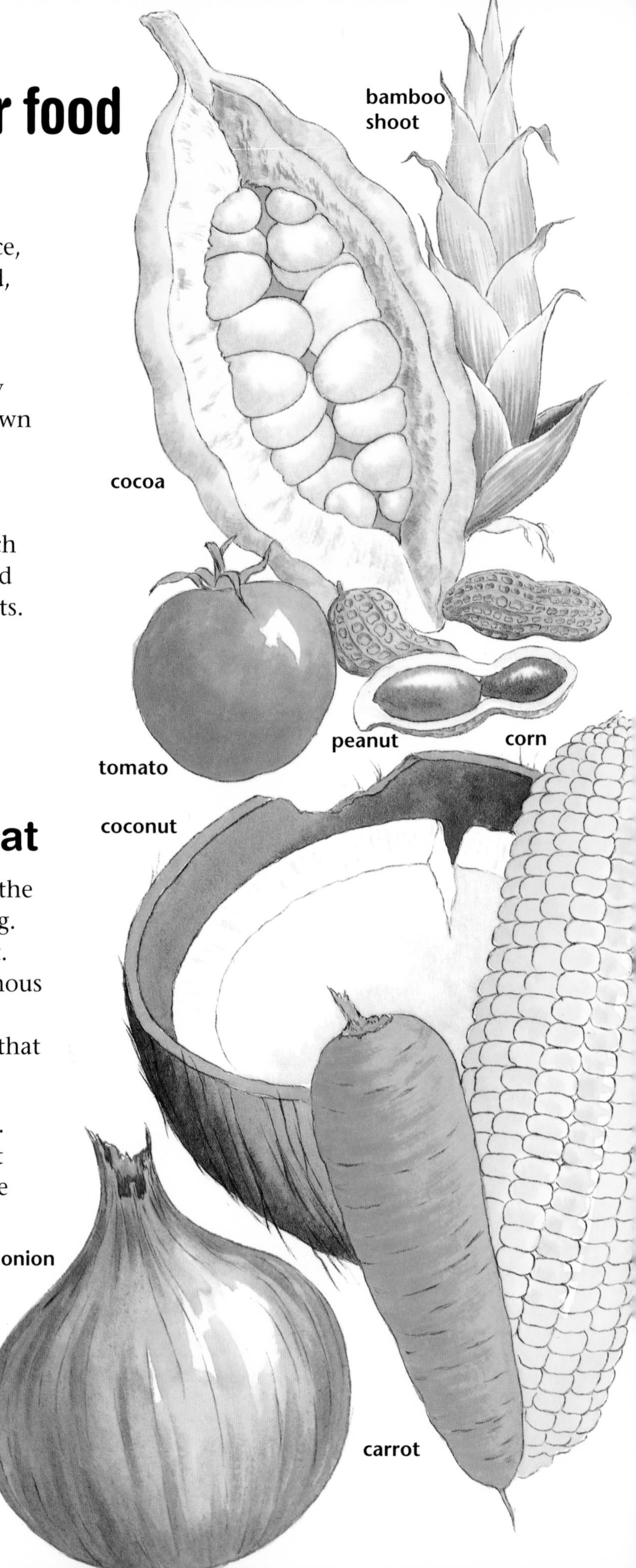

These foods have one thing in common—they come from plants.

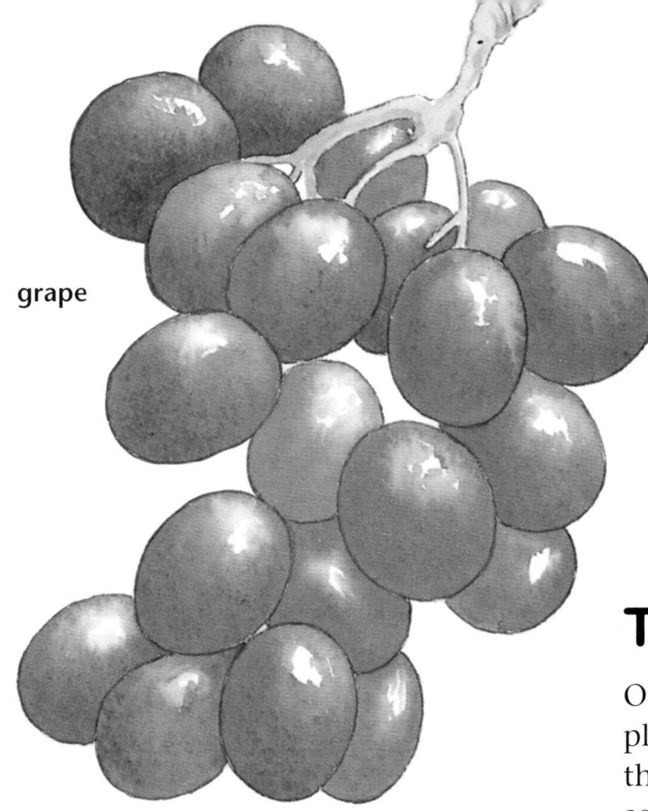
grape

Find out more by looking at pages **88–89**
94–95

The biggest and best

Our ancestors discovered long ago which plants or parts of plants could be eaten, and they began to grow as many different plants as they could. During each harvest they tried to choose the biggest and best plants to provide seeds for the next crop. In this way, the quality of the crops gradually improved. Today's carrots, for example, are much bigger and sweeter than the wild ones that our ancestors discovered hundreds of years ago.

Drinks such as tea and coffee come from plants. Here, workers in Java pick the young leaves from tea plants.

Do you eat grass?

Can you name four different animals that eat grass? Horses, sheep, cattle, and deer eat grass. Eating grass from the ground is called **grazing**, and the animals that feed in this way are called **grazers.**

Did you know that most human beings depend on grasses for their daily food? Of course, human beings are not grazers. We don't go out into the fields and chew grass straight from the ground, like the animals mentioned above! But we do grow grass plants, such as wheat, rice, barley, millet, and sugar cane. We use the seeds of wheat to make flour for bread and cakes. We cook and eat the seeds of rice, barley, and millet. And we squeeze the juice from sugar cane and use it to make some of our drinks and foods taste sweeter. We also use sugar to feed the yeast that helps to make our bread.

The seeds of grasses are full of a substance called **starch.** This starch is the seed's own food supply when it first starts to grow. But starch is a good food for human beings, too. Starch can give us much of the energy we need to live.

Grass plants have matted roots that take in moisture from the top layer of the soil. The plants produce new leaves and shoots after the old ones have been eaten by grazing animals.

More than half the world's sugar supply comes from the sugar cane plant.

We use grass to make bread!

Bread is usually made with flour, sugar, yeast, and water. Flour comes from wheat, and sugar comes from sugar cane. Wheat and sugar are two different kinds of grass plants. So we use grass to make bread!

The yeast makes the bread "rise." Yeast makes a gas called carbon dioxide as it feeds on sugar and multiplies. Carbon dioxide is the same gas that makes the bubbles in fizzy drinks, such as soda pop. When yeast feeds on sugar, the carbon dioxide it produces makes a bubbly froth that works with the flour to make the bread rise and expand. Yeast can feed on sugar only when it's kept in a warm place.

Find out more by looking at pages **78–79**

Fun with yeast

You will need:

self-adhesive labels

a felt-tipped pen

water

teaspoon and 1/2-teaspoon measuring spoons

4 1/2 teaspoons of sugar

four small glass jars

4 1/2 teaspoons of yeast, either fresh or dried

1. Number your jars, 1, 2, 3, and 4. Put 1/2 teaspoon of yeast into jar 1, and fill the jar halfway with warm water.

2. Put 1/2 teaspoon of sugar into jars 2, 3, and 4. Fill jar 2 halfway with warm water.

3. Add 1/2 teaspoon of yeast to jars 3 and 4. Fill jar 3 halfway with warm water, and fill jar 4 halfway with cold water.

4. Put jars 1, 2, and 3 in a warm place, such as on a sunny window sill or near an oven. Put jar 4 in a cold place, such as a refrigerator. Leave the jars for three or four hours.

Can you guess what will happen? The yeast can only feed on the sugar in one of the jars—do you know which jar this will be? Do the experiment and see if you were right.

Healing plants

Gardeners grow flowers for their beauty. Farmers grow vegetables and other plants to feed people and animals. But plants are also important for another reason. Many plants are used as medicine.

For hundreds of years, people have known that some plants can treat illnesses. Up until this century, most drugs were made from plant parts. Today, about one-quarter of all the medicines people take still come from plants.

More than 400 years ago, Spanish explorers in South America discovered that the people living there used the bark of the cinchona tree to reduce fever. The bark is still used to make **quinine**, a drug used to treat malaria and other diseases.

Digitalis is another medicine that comes from a plant. Drug manufacturers make digitalis from the dried leaves of the purple foxglove plant. It is used to treat heart disease.

Medicine made from plants has saved many lives. The roots of the **ipecac** plant are used to make syrup of ipecac, which is used to treat poisoning.

The foxglove plant is used to make digitalis, a medicine used to treat heart disease.

The bark of the cinchona tree is used to make quinine, a drug used to treat malaria and other diseases.

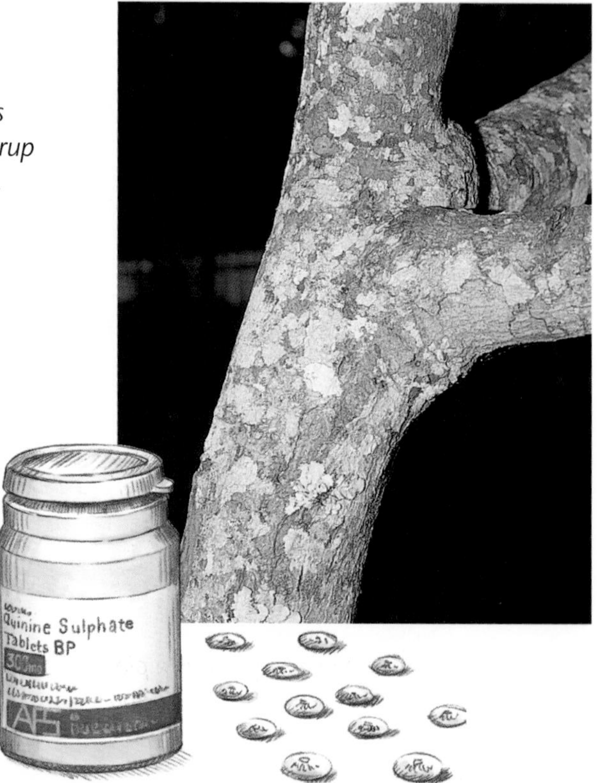

The ipecac plant is used to make a syrup to treat poisoning.

Feeling better with plants

Medicine made from plants treat and cure disease, and they can help people relieve aches, pains, and itching, too.

The autumn crocus contains something called colchicine, which helps reduce joint swelling in people with arthritis. The oil of the camphor tree is used in lotions to relieve pain and itching.

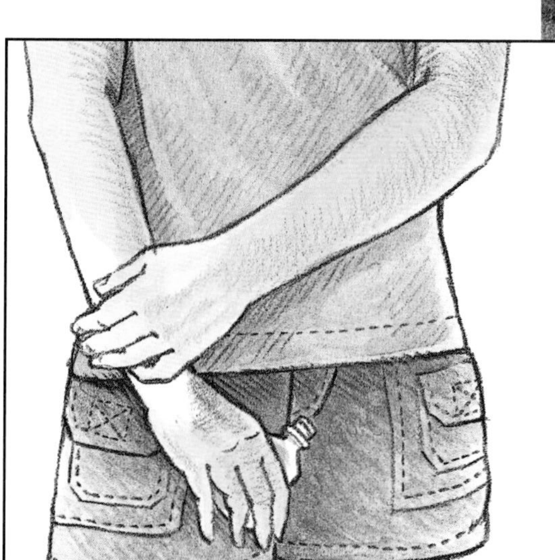

The oil of the camphor tree is used to make lotions to relieve pain and itching.

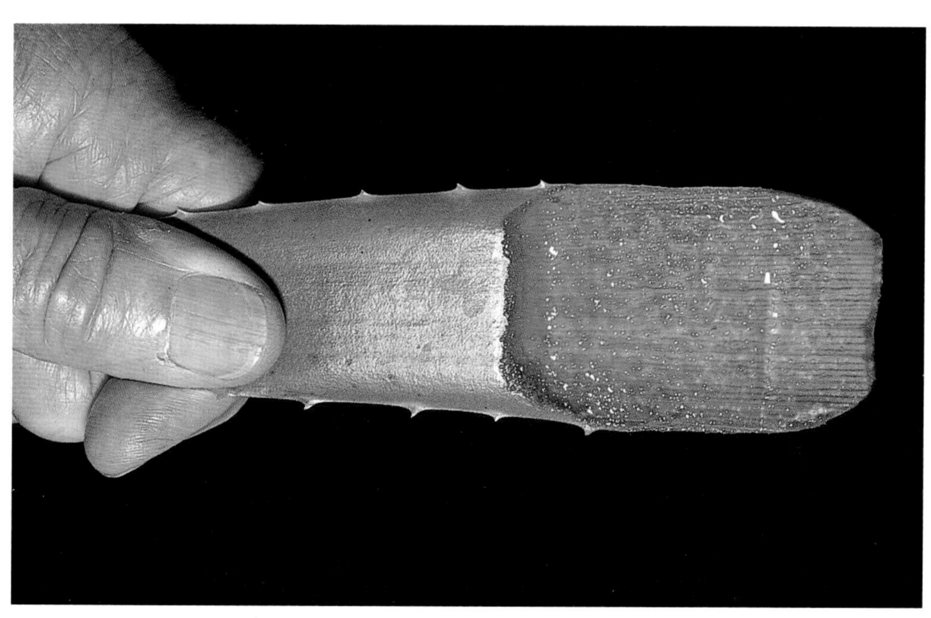

Many people keep an aloe plant near their kitchen stove. The juice inside the long leaves of this plant can be applied to burns for quick pain relief.

Plants in danger

Life on Earth would not be possible without plants. The oxygen we breathe comes from plants. The food we eat comes from plants or from animals that eat plants. Medicine from plant parts treat many diseases. Many of our buildings are made of wood, which comes from plants. Are you wearing a cotton shirt today? That's made of fibers from the cotton plant!

Because we use plants in so many ways, it's very important to protect their habitats. When people manage, protect, and wisely use plants and all the things that support life on Earth, it is called **conservation.** People who work to protect plants, animals, and the earth from destruction are called **conservationists.**

In many parts of the world, many plants are in danger of extinction because too many forests are being cut down. Animals, such as cattle, goats, and sheep, which have been allowed to overgraze plants in their pastures, are killing off plants and preventing seed formation to make new plants. Some coastal swamps have been filled in with earth to make room for building.

Plants are in danger of extinction in many parts of the world because forests are being cut down.

Some coastal swamps have been filled in to make room for houses.

Preserving plants

There are many ways people conserve plants. When lumber companies replant areas of forests where they have cut timber, that is conservation. When ranchers move their animals from pasture to pasture, new plants are allowed to grow. This is called **grazing rotation.** Controlled burning of grasslands encourages new plant growth, too.

Lumber companies help conserve plants by replanting areas of forests where they have cut timber.

Glossary

Absorption: The process through which a plant takes in water and nutrients.

Angiosperm: A flowering plant; one of the two groups of seed plants.

Animal: Living thing that eats plants or other animals, and usually can move around. Animals are one of the five *kingdoms*.

Annual: Plant that grows and dies in one year.

Biennial: Plant that needs two years to grow, flower, and die.

Blood: Fluid that travels around the bodies of animals, carrying food and oxygen to cells and taking away wastes.

Botanist: Scientist who studies plants.

Breathing: Process of taking in and releasing certain gases. Almost all living things must breathe.

Bryophyte: A small, nonflowering plant that lacks tissue to carry water and food throughout its body.

Carbon: Element found in all living things.

Carbon dioxide: Gas used by plants in *photosynthesis*.

Carnivore: Animal that eats meat.

Cell: Basic unit of life. Every living thing is made up of at least one cell.

Chaparral: A region of scrubs and small trees that occurs in areas with hot, dry summers and cool, wet winters.

Chlorophyll: Green substance in plant cells that uses energy from sunlight to make food.

Chloroplast: Working part of a plant cell that accomplishes photosynthesis.

Classify: Sort things into groups according to how they are alike.

Conifer: Cone-bearing tree or shrub.

Conservation: The management, protection, and wise use of plants, animals, and other natural resources.

Deciduous tree: Tree whose leaves change color and fall every year.

Decomposition: Process by which a dead plant or animal *decays*, or breaks down into smaller and simpler pieces.

Desert: Dry region with very little rain.

Digestion: Process by which a living thing breaks down food into pieces it can absorb.

Embryo: New plant or animal formed by the union of a male reproductive cell and a female reproductive cell.

Enzyme: Chemical in the body that helps break down food.

Epiphyte: A plant that grows on another plant but makes its own food.

Evergreen tree: Tree with leaves that stay green all year.

Exoskeleton: Hard outer casing of animals such as insects, that gives shape to them.

Food chain: Process of food energy passing from plants to animals.

Fossilized: Turned to stone.

Fruit: Part of a flowering plant that contains the plant's seeds.

Fungus: Living thing, such as a mushroom, that feeds off living and rotting plants; fungi make up one of the five kingdoms of living things.

Germination: Sprouting of a new plant from a seed.

Gymnosperm: A seed plant that does not have flowers. It produces naked or uncovered seeds.

Habitat: Place to live.

Herbivore: Animal that eats plants.

Hormone: Chemical substance that helps to control such body functions as growth, development, and reproduction.

Humus: Part of the soil made of material that was once alive.

Kingdom: One of the large groups into which biologists divide living things.

Lycophyte: A plant whose leaves have a single, central vein. Lycophytes include club mosses (which are not true mosses) and quillworts.

Natural selection: The process by which a species of plant or animal changes its features over a long period of time in order for the species to survive in its environment.

Nervous system: Network of nerve cells that pass messages between the brain and other parts of an animal.

Nonvascular plant: A plant that lacks a vascular system.

Nucleus: Center of an atom. A nucleus is made of tiny particles called *protons* and *neutrons.*

Nutrient: Substance, such as nitrogen, that makes a plant or animal grow.

Omnivore: Animal that eats both plants and animals.

Ovary: The female reproductive cell. In plants, it contains the *ovules*, which become seeds.

Oxygen: Gas needed by all living things.

Parasite: Animal or plant that lives on the plant or animal on which it feeds.

Perennial: Plant that grows and flowers for many years.

Photosynthesis: Process by which green plants make their own food.

Plankton: Mass of algae, protozoans, and tiny animals, often forming a sheet over a body of water.

Plant: Living thing that makes its own food. Plants make up one of the five kingdoms.

Pollen: Grain that carries a plant's sperm.

Pollination: Transfer of *pollen*—and sperm—from one flower to the *ovary* of another flower of the same kind.

Prokaryotes: Tiny living things, mostly bacteria. Prokaryotes make up one of the five kingdoms.

Protein: One of the chemical substances that exist in every cell and are essential to plant and animal life.

Protist: Tiny living thing, such as an ameba. Protists make up one of the five kingdoms.

Rain forest: Dense forest in a hot, wet area.

Reproduction: Process by which living things make copies of themselves.

Root: Part of a plant that grows downward. Roots hold the plant in place and absorb water and nutrients from the soil.

Seed: Plant embryo protected by an outer cover.

Shoot: Part of new plant that grows upward.

Soil: Mixture of *organic material*—material that was once alive—and *inorganic material*—material never alive.

Sperm: Male reproductive cell.

Splitting: Method of reproduction in which the adult cell splits into two new cells.

Spore: Single cell that sprouts into a new plant.

Stomata: Tiny openings in a plant's leaves through which oxygen, water vapor, and other gases move.

Succulent: A fleshy plant, such as a cactus, that has large stems or leaves in which water is stored.

Transpiration: Process by which water travels through a plant, carrying nutrients and food.

Tundra: Cold, dry region where no trees grow.

Vascular plant: A plant that has a vascular system, which allows it to absorb water and other nutrients throughout its body.

Vegetarian: Person who eats food only from plants.

Index

Page numbers in *italic* type are references to illustrations.

D

E

F

M

N

O

P

Acknowledgements

The publishers of **World Book's** *Young Scientist* acknowledge the following photographers, publishers, agencies, and corporations for photographs used in this volume.

Cover © PhotoDisc, Inc.
2/3 © PhotoDisc, Inc.
8/9 © Breck P. Kent, Earth Scenes; © Norman Myers, Bruce Coleman Collection
10/11 © Jane Burton, Bruce Coleman Collection
18/19 © Eric Grave, Science Photo Library
22/23 © Michael Abbey, Science Photo Library
24/25 © C. Carvalho, Frank Lane Picture Agency
26/27 © Tony Brain and David Parker from Science Photo Library
28/29 © Michael Chinery; © Jana R. Jirak; © C. P. Armstrong
32/33 © Avril Ramage, Oxford Scientific Films
34/35 © Reinhard, ZEFA Picture Library
36/37 © Michael Chinery; © Bruce Coleman Collection
38/39 © Peter Ward, Bruce Coleman Collection
40/41 © Jeff Simon, Bruce Coleman Collection
42/43 © A. Wharton, Frank Lane Picture Agency
52/53 © Jane Burton, Bruce Coleman Collection; © CNRI from Science Photo Library
54/55 © Kim Taylor, Bruce Coleman Collection; © Eric Crichton, Bruce Coleman Collection
56/57 © Kim Taylor, Bruce Coleman Collection
58/59 © John Cancalosi, Bruce Coleman Collection; © Sinclair Stammer, Science Photo Library
66/67 © John Shaw, Bruce Coleman Collection
68/69 © L. C. Marigo, Bruce Coleman Collection
70/71 © Roger Tidman, Frank Lane Picture Agency; © J. Wisniewski, Frank Lane Picture Agency; © Michael Chinery
72/73 © William E. Townsend, Jr., Bruce Coleman Collection; © Michael Chinery
74/75 © Michael Chinery
76/77 © Doug Wechsler, Earth Scenes; © Patti Murray, Earth Scenes
78/79 © Peter Davey, Bruce Coleman Collection
82/83 © ZEFA Picture Library
90/91 © Eric Crichton, Bruce Coleman Collection
94/95 © Bruce Coleman Inc.
98–107 © Michael Chinery
108/109 © Zig Leszczynski, Earth Scenes
110/111 © Michael Freeman, Bruce Coleman Collection
112/113 © Eric Crichton, Bruce Coleman Collection; © Michael Chinery
114/115 © Richard Shiell, Earth Scenes; © Jesse M. Harris; © E. F. Anderson, Visuals Unlimited; © Fred Whitehead, Earth Scenes; © Michel Viard, Peter Arnold, Inc.
116/117 © George Godfrey, Earth Scenes; © Jeff Foott, Bruce Coleman Inc.; © Mark Godfrey, The Image Works

Illustrated by

Martin Aitchinson
Nigel Alexander
Hemesh Alles
Martyn Andrews
Sue Barclay
Richard Berridge
John Booth
Lou Bory
Maggie Brand
Stephen Brayfield
Bristol Illustrators
Colin Brown
Estelle Carol
David Cook
Marie DeJohn
Richard Deverell
Farley, White and Veal
Sheila Galbraith
Peter Geissler
Jeremy Gower
Kathie Kelleher
Stuart Lafford
John Lobban
Louise Martin
Annabel Milne
Yoshi Miyake
Donald Moss
Eileen Mueller Neill
Teresa O'Brien
Paul Perreault
Roberta Polfus
Jeremy Pyke
Trevor Ridley
Barry Rowe
Don Simpson
Gary Slater
Lawrie Taylor
Gwen Tourret
Pat Tourret
Peter Visscher
David Webb
Gerald Whitcomb
Matthew White
Lynne Willey